World in a Nu

Enisen Publishing

Islam in a Nutshell

*Flag: The star and crescent symbol actually predates Islam by several thousand years. Once used to symbolize sun, moon and sky gods worshipped by people of Central Asia and Siberia, the crescent was adopted by the city of Byzantium (modern-day Istanbul) in commemoration of the goddess Diana. When Byzantium (later called Constantinople) became Christian, the city was rededicated to the Virgin Mary whose star symbol was added to the crescent. When Muslim Ottoman Turks invaded in 1453, they adopted the city's flag and symbols which came to identify Islam – the crescent moon symbolizing Islam's use of the lunar calendar, the five points of the star signifying the Five Pillars of Islam.

The tribes of the early Muslim community used simple solid-colored flags in battle for identification purposes only.

Many thanks to:
Berj Boyajian, Professor of Comparative Islamic Law
Masood Behshid
Hamid Zavosh

Islam in a Nutshell
First edition – April 2002
First published – April 2002
Second edition – September 2004

Enisen Publishing
2118 Wilshire Blvd. #351
Santa Monica, CA 90403-5784
http://www.enisen.com
publishing@enisen.com

Text	Amanda Roraback
Maps	Katie Gerber
Editor	Paul Bernhard
Editor-in-Chief	Dorothy A. Roraback

"Islam in a Nutshell" and all Nutshell Notes books
made possible by the generous support of Avo Tavitian

ISBN # 0-9702908-8-8

Library of Congress Control Number: 2004111752

Printed in the United States of America

TABLE OF CONTENTS

ARABIA IN THE TIME OF MUHAMMED

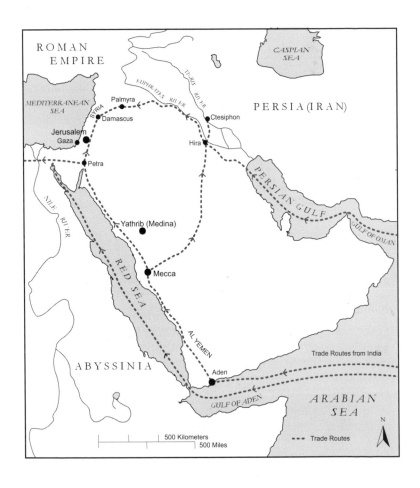

THE LIFE OF MOHAMMED

ARABIA IN THE 6TH CENTURY

Arabia, home of Islam's most holy cities, birthplace of Islam's founder (the **Prophet Mohammed**) and the destination of millions of Muslims performing the required pilgrimage to Mecca each year is a large desert peninsula

Despite its harsh environment, land routes across the peninsula and along its waterways were invaluable to traders transporting goods between India and China and the Mediterranean markets in the 6th century A.D., particularly since fighting between the Persian and Roman Empires in Egypt, Syria and Iraq had made travel along the northern routes a perilous venture. While the two superpowers battled for dominance, commercial activity in the relatively stable Arabian Peninsula flourished. As a result, the oasis cities catering to caravans carrying frankincense and myrrh[1] from Arabia to Roman markets along the so-called "incense route," prospered.

One of the most notable caravan cities of the time, **Mecca**, was known for its trade fairs, festivals and contests pitting poets from all parts of Arabia against each other in literary competition. Mecca's biggest source of commerce, though, came from visitors traveling to its main attraction: a large black meteorite housed in a box-shaped building (the **Ka'aba** or "Cube").

ABRAHAM

According to Muslims, 4,000 years ago, the Prophet Abraham was instructed by God to bring his servant, **Hagar**, and their son, **Ishmael** to Arabia from Palestine to assuage the jealousy of his once-barren wife, **Sarah** (see section The Bible and the Qur'an) .

Because **Sarah** was unable to have children, Abraham bedded her servant **Hagar** who bore him a son called **Ishmael**. Abraham loved his child deeply but his loyalty to God was even stronger. Therefore, when the Prophet Abraham was instructed by God to sacrifice his beloved son to show his devotion, Abraham mournfully but dutifully obeyed. Just as he was about to strike his child dead, though, an angel appeared to tell him that he had passed God's test and his son's life should be spared.

As a reward for his piety, Abraham was granted a second son, **Isaac**, born to his by now elderly wife, Sarah.

However, after the birth of Isaac, Sarah became jealous of Hagar and Ishmael. Abraham was compelled by Sarah to send them away to the uninhabited city of Baca (Mecca's original name) and left them there with limited provisions.

---

[1] The highly prized spices could only be obtained from trees growing in southern Arabia, Ethiopia and Somalia

When the two ran out of water, Hagar raced back and forth in panic until a water-spring miraculously began to gush from the ground under Ishmael's feet (the location of the **Zam Zam Well**). Mother and son had been saved and the water was traded with nomadic tribes for food.

Some time later, Abraham returned to Mecca and helped his son build a shrine around the meteorite (the forerunner of the present-day **Ka'aba**) which was to become a gathering place for all those who wished to strengthen their faith in God.

Centuries later the Ka'aba was turned into a house in which to store statues representing more than three hundred deities. Each year, tens of thousands of pagans would gather in Mecca from all over Arabia to ceremoniously circumambulate the stone and worship idols.

For three months surrounding the sacred period of pilgrimage, all fighting was forbidden in order to allow the worshippers safe passage (and also permitting trade to take place without threat of bandits).

The resourceful Meccans used the opportunity to sell goods at giant trade fairs that took place some weeks before the pilgrimage season. Preservation of the Ka'aba and its spiritual significance was vital for the cities financial survival.

TRIBAL SOCIETY

The inhabitants of Arabia were divided into two groups: the Bedouin nomads who wandered the desert in search of fresh grazing grass for their camels, sheep and goats, and the oasis-dwellers who relied on trade and agriculture for their survival.

Both groups were organized into close-knit tribes and followed strict codes of honor. In this way, Arabia, a country too poor to have a government, laws or a police force, had developed its own sense of order. In place of a court system, inter-tribal crimes were avenged by blood feuds and local matters were resolved through democratic tribal deliberations or decided by employed arbitrators believed to have supernatural abilities. A person's loyalty to his tribe was necessary for self-preservation.

QURAISH TRIBE

In Mecca, the most powerful tribe, the **Quraish**, was entrusted with the city's most important and prestigious job, tending the Ka'aba. Each Quraish clan member was appointed to a particular duty that would be passed on from generation to generation. The **Hashim** clan (or Banu Hashim), for instance, was charged with feeding the pilgrims and providing water from the **Zam Zam Well**. It was into this clan in about AD 570[2] that **Muhammed,** the future prophet and founder of Islam, was born.

---

[2] The actual date of Muhammed's birth is debated.

MUHAMMED'S EARLY LIFE

A few months after his son was conceived in the city of **Yathrib** (later called **Medina**), Muhammed's father, **Abdullah**,[3] died. His mother, **Amina**, died when Muhammed was six years old leaving the orphan to live with his paternal grandfather, **Abd-al-Muttalib** (a leader of the prestigious **Hashim** clan). When his grandfather died two years later, Muhammed was finally placed under the care of his beloved uncle **Abu Talib**[4] — who had then become the new leader of the Hashim clan.

In his youth, Muhammed accompanied his uncle on commercial caravan trips to Syria where he gained trading experience and began to learn about Christianity, Judaism and foreign cultures.

When he was twenty five years old, he was hired to lead the caravan of a rich 40-year old widow named **Khadija**. After her husband's death, Khadija had maintained his caravan trade and became a successful businesswoman. Impressed with Muhammed's skill and honesty, she soon asked him to marry her and, despite her advanced age, bore Muhammed six children: two sons (who died in infancy) and four daughters. For the next 25 years, Muhammed was faithful to his wife, whom he adored and cherished.

Between A.D. 595 and A.D. 610, Muhammed lived a tranquil life in Mecca doing business and periodically meditating in caves around the city. To repay his aging uncle, **Abu Talib**, for his guardianship in Muhammed's youth, the future prophet took in his uncle's son, **Ali**, and raised him as his own child.

FIRST REVELATION

As the years passed, Muhammed became weary of worldly concerns and devoted an increasing amount of time in quiet meditation. One night, in the month of **Ramadan**, a vision came to him. An angel (**Gabriel**) sent from God announced that he had been chosen to be the last messenger of God (**Allah**). Frightened by such an awe-inspiring spectacle, Muhammed ran home and trembled until Khadija's comfort prompted him to recount his experience. Khadija, at that moment, had become Muhammed's first convert. The second was his cousin, **Ali**.

The revelation he received that night was the first in a series of oracles he would receive in his lifetime, which would eventually be compiled into Islam's holy book, the **Qur'an** (or **Koran**). When the angel instructed Muhammed to "warn people and collect them to God," the prophet began to

---

[3] The prefix "abd" in Arabic means "servant of." The name Abdullah can therefore be translated as "Servant of Allah (God)." The notion of "Allah" existed in the Meccan pantheon long before Islam but his singular divine status wasn't acknowledged until after Muhammed.

[4] The Arabic prefix "abu" means "father of" taken by parents after the birth of their first son. The female version is "umm."

preach publicly and gather followers. **Abu Bakr**, a prosperous merchant and one of Muhammed's most loyal companions, became one of the most active proselytizers.

Initially, as has been the case in most religions, the movement attracted young and poor adherents who didn't enjoy the protection of powerful tribal associations. But as the movement grew to other circles, the Meccans became concerned.

MECCANS RESPONSE
Muhammed offended the pagan Meccans by denouncing their gods and insulting their ancestors by claiming they would all be punished with hellfire for worshipping idols in place of the one true God.

The leaders of Quraish were also concerned that Muhammed's preaching would one day lead to the de-sanctification of the **Ka'aba**, the cornerstone of the tribe's prestige and the source of the city's prosperity.

But one of the most objectionable concepts was Muhammed's belief that, regardless of blood and familial affiliation, his followers were all brothers under God. Muhammed's Muslim brotherhood (or ***umma***) cut across tribal lines pitting the faithful against their pagan family members.

PERSECUTION OF MUSLIMS
To try to curb Muhammed's activity, the Meccans imposed sanctions against all members of the **Hashim** clan and forbade other clans and tribes from buying or selling goods to them. Meccan families also doled out punishments against their own converted family members and slaves and taunted Muslim adherents.

In the year 619 Muhammed suffered a double blow with the deaths of his beloved wife and of his favorite uncle and supporter, **Abu Talib**. When another uncle, **Abu Lahab**, one of the prophet's most bitter enemies, took over as head of the **Hashim** clan, Muhammed also lost the tribal protection he had received under the tutelage of Abu Talib.

FLIGHT TO JERUSALEM
In that same year, Muhammed took his famous "flight to Jerusalem." Accompanied by the angel **Gabriel**, Muhammed was taken on a celestial journey to the **Temple Mount** in Jerusalem,[5] where he ascended the seven

---

[5] In Sura 17:1, the Qur'an says *Glorified and Exalted be He (Allah) who took His servant for a journey by night from the Sacred Mosque ("Masjid Al-Haram"* [interpreted to mean the mosque in **Mecca**]) *to the Far Away Mosque ("Masjid Al-Aqsa"* [interpreted by Muslims to mean **Jerusalem**]*).* The omission of the name "Jerusalem" has led critics to doubt Muslim claims that the city and the Temple (upon which is built the "Dome of the Rock" commemorating the spot where Muhammed had taken his first step to heaven, and the "Al-Aqsa Mosque") holds significant spiritual value. (See Roraback, Israel-Palestine in a Nutshell, Enisen Publishing, 2004 for more information)

heavens, meeting Biblical patriarchs along the way. After praying with **Adam, Abraham, Joseph, Enoch, Aaron** and **Moses**, Abraham reached the seventh heaven, where he asked **Jesus** to introduce him to God.

The next day, Muhammed reported to his followers that he had been given a glimpse of the heavens and had received instructions from God regarding the prayers his followers should perform.

HIJRAH

The hostility that faced Muhammed and his followers in Mecca after the deaths of **Khadija** and **Abu Talib** convinced the Prophet it was time to leave the city.

For two years Muhammed and his followers met with idolaters from the city of **Yathrib** who had come to Mecca on their yearly pilgrimage to the Ka'aba. After several visits, the Muslims won their trust and Muhammed was invited to act as an arbiter between two rival tribes.

> The year 622 has been designated the official starting point of the Muslim era and the first year in the Islamic calendar. The calendar year normally lasts 354 days (leap years are 355 days) composed of 12 lunar months.

After a harrowing escape, the Prophet and his followers moved north to the lush agricultural oasis in A.D. 622. From that point on, the city of **Yathrib** was known as the Prophet's City or "Medinat al Nebi" (shortened to **Medina**).

MEDINA

Muhammed expected that he and his Muslim followers would be well received in Medina since the town was inhabited and dominated by Jewish tribes and the two religions were very similar. For example, Muhammed instructed his followers to face toward Jerusalem when they prayed and Muslim dietary laws were comparable to the Jewish Kosher requirements: no consumption of pork; the draining of all blood from meat before it was cooked and eaten. Because Muhammed was considered the last in a line of prophets sent down with the same message as his predecessors (Abraham, Moses, Jesus, et al.) the revelations compiled in the Qur'an included many of those found in the Jewish Torah and Christian Bible. The accounts of God's creations, Adam and Eve, Noah's ark and Abraham's sacrifice to God, for instance, were all included in the pages of the Qur'an, albeit with minor adjustments (for example, Muslims believe that Abraham was asked to sacrifice Ishmael, Hagar's son, rather than Isaac, his second born).

But rather than receiving Muhammed as a Messenger or the promised Messiah, the Jewish scholars challenged his knowledge of biblical history.

With their incessant cross-questioning, they tried to make the Prophet appear ignorant and ridiculous.

The friction that continued to grow between the Jews and the Muslims eventually drove Muhammed to adjust Islamic rituals to distinguish the Muslims from the Jews. The direction of prayer (*qibla*) was changed from Jerusalem to Mecca, the duration of fasting was lengthened from 10 days (in the Jewish tradition) to 30 days, and the special Muslim day of prayer was changed from Saturday (the Jewish Sabbath) to Friday – although unlike the Jews, the Muslims didn't consider Friday a "day of rest," since they contend that God never had to rest after he created the heavens and the earth. (see section The Bible and the Qur'an)

CARAVAN RAIDS
Before his migration to Medina, Muhammed had received a message from God permitting the Muslims to fight for the preservation of the faith. Furthermore, those who died while fighting in the service of Islam would be instantly admitted to Paradise as martyrs.

When the Meccans continued to threaten the Muslims, therefore, Muhammed felt justified conducting raids against the caravans led by his enemies as they passed Medina on the way to Syria.

After winning some victories (the **Battle of Badr**) and suffering some setbacks (at **Uhud**, for instance) the Muslims began to grow into a capable fighting force buttressed by converts from neighboring tribes. With the spoils won during successful raids, moreover, the Muslims had become wealthy, powerful and prestigious.

RETURN TO MECCA
Eight years after the Muslim exodus to Medina, there was an opportune time to win back the city of Mecca. When the Quraish broke a treaty made in A.D. 628 (the **Treaty of Hudaybiyya**) that allowed the Muslims safe entry into the city to perform their pilgrimmage, Muhammed and his entourage entered forcefully.

The venerated Prophet rode into the city with 10,000 of his followers, performed the ritual seven circuits around the **Ka'aba**, and methodically smashed all 360 idols that had been placed around the sacred stone. At the Ka'aba, Muhammed declared that there is no god but God (**Allah**) and that he, **Muhammed**, was his Prophet.

Without coercion, the people of Mecca gathered around Muhammed and one by one pledged allegiance to God and his Messenger.

By the time of his death in A.D. 632, almost all the tribes of Arabia had converted to Islam and joined the Muslim community (*umma*).

RIGHTLY GUIDED CALIPHS

Muhammed had not designated a successor before he became ill although he had delegated some functions from his deathbed, such as the call to prayer, to his closest companions.[6] The decision of a successor was left to his followers who gathered shortly after the Prophet passed away (A.D. 632) to decide who would lead the community of believers (*umma*) in Muhammed's place.

After heated debate at the *shura* (a meeting of companions who had been elected in the Prophet's lifetime),[7] it was decided that **Abu Bakr**, the Prophet's closest friend and one of the first converts, would become the first **Caliph** (successor).

ABU BAKR (632-634)

Immediately after his appointment, **Abu Bakr** turned his attention to Muslim rule in the Arabian Peninsula. After Muhammed's death, several tribes who had previously accepted Islam because it was popular or as a fulfillment of a political pact, declared that they would no longer pay their *zakat* taxes or perform other Islamic duties. Compounding the situation, Medina was being besieged by Arab Bedouins.

In a string of minor wars known as the **Wars of Apostasy (Riddah), Abu Bakr** crushed the tribal revolts and consolidated Muslim rule over the entire Arabian Peninsula.

In the same year (A.D. 633) the first **Caliph** also sent an army of 8,000 men to engage in a defensive battle against the Persians, who had been backing the Bedouin rebels in hopes of bringing down the Muslim empire. After a series of victories, the Muslims captured huge areas of the western Persian Empire.

Two years after a whirlwind of further military victories against the Persians and the Byzantines, **Abu Bakr** fell ill. By his suggestion **Umar ibn al Khattab**[8] was selected to lead the community as Islam's second "**Rightly Guided Caliphs.**"

UMAR IBN AL KHATTAB (634-644)

Under the leadership of Umar, one of Muhammed's first companions, Muslim rule had been consolidated over Palestine, Syria, Egypt and Iraq and Arabic began to replace such ancient languages of the Near East as Aramaic

---

[6] According to some Sunni historians, when Muhammed became sick and couldn't act as the prayer leader he asked **Abu Bakr** to perform the duty. The account was put forth as proof that the dying Prophet wanted him to be his successor. According to other historians, however, Muhammed assigned a black former slave called **Bilal** to call the faithful to prayer.

[7] The Shi'as believe that only God had the power to choose a successor to Muhammed.

[8] In Arabic the prefix "ibn" means "son of." The female version "bint" means "daughter of."

(the language Jesus spoke) and Coptic. After decades of conflict, the two superpowers of the time (Persians and Byzantines) were too weak to resist the fresh Muslim armies. In fact, the Christians of Byzantium welcomed liberation by the Arabs once they felt assured that no harm would come to them and that they would be allowed to practice their religion freely under Muslim rule.

As he lay dying from a knife wound delivered by a Persian assassin, **Umar** appointed an "election committee" to select his successor. After consultation, the council chose **Uthman ibn Affan**.

UTHMAN IBN AFFAN (644-656)
Uthman, who was a member of the **Umayyad clan**, a leading Meccan family, built the first Muslim navy and authorized the first canonical compilation of the **Qur'an** (a version still in use today).

But although Uthman was a pious and gentle man, his authority was bitterly opposed because of his background (the **Umayyad** family had been among the Prophet's strongest foes) and his inability to curb rampant corruption that had erupted among Muslim governors.

Before long, tribal factionalism and the threat of rebellion had resurfaced in the community and in A.D. 656, Uthman was murdered by a group of mutineers from Egypt.

ALI IBN ABI TALIB (656-661)
After the death of the third of the "Rightly Guided Caliphs," the election committee finally turned to **Ali ibn Abi Talib**, Muhammed's cousin ("ibn" or "son of" **Abu Talib**) who was married to the Prophet's only living daughter **Fatima**.

Along with the position as military and political leader of the *ummah*, Ali also inherited the problems plaguing the Muslim nation. Corrupt governors continued to rule, and mobs of Muslims eager to punish **Uthman's** killers, rose up in anger.

On the question of Uthman's murder, **Ali** decided to delay his investigation until the situation was better understood. His hesitation, though, was interpreted as a refusal to bring the killers to justice and resulted in two opposition movements challenging his authority.

One group was headed by Muhammed's widow **Aisha** (Muhammed's third wife and the daughter of **Abu Bakr**) and the other by **Mu'awiya**, the governor of Syria and **Uthman's** nephew.

In the course of the **Battle of the Camel** (so named because it took place around a camel that Aisha had ridden into the battlefield) the rebels went to the city of Basra in search of Uthman's killers and gathered an army large enough to overthrow Medina. When news reached Ali, he organized an army of his own to stop Aisha and her supporters. After a chaotic battle,

Ali's army defeated the rebels and peace was restored.

Ali was now free to deal with the corrupt governors. Believing Uthman's appointees to be weak and undependable, Ali decided to replace them all. But **Mu'awiya**, Uthman's relative, refused to step down. Instead, the Syrian governor made a bid for the Caliphate in an insurrection culminating in the prolonged **Battle of Siffin** (AD 657).

The Battle of Siffin dragged on without a conclusion for several months[9] compelling Ali to accept **Mu'awiya's** proposal to appoint the next Caliph through arbitration.

Ali's willingness to readily resolve their differences by arbitrating what his supporters believed was his rightful entitlement to the Caliphate, though, had so enraged a group of Ali's followers that they separated into their own radical faction called the **Kharijites** ("seceders") (see chapter Sects and Offshoots) and plotted the death of both **Ali** and **Mu'awiya**. Ali's murder was successfully carried out by a lone Kharijite assassin (Mu'awiya escaped) and his eldest son, **Hassan**, became Caliph. After a few months Hassan was forced to cede the Caliphate to Mu'awiya under threat of violence.

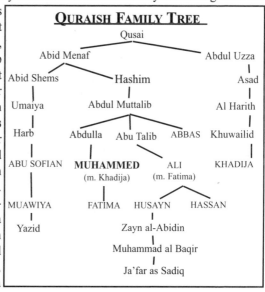

QURAISH FAMILY TREE

Qusai — Abid Menaf — Abdul Uzza; Abid Menaf — Abid Shems, Hashim; Abdul Uzza — Asad; Abid Shems — Umaiya — Harb — ABU SOFIAN — MUAWIYA — Yazid; Hashim — Abdul Muttalib — Abdulla, Abu Talib, ABBAS; Abdulla — MUHAMMED (m. Khadija) — FATIMA; Abu Talib — ALI (m. Fatima) — HUSAYN, HASSAN; Asad — Al Harith — Khuwailid — KHADIJA; HUSAYN — Zayn al-Abidin — Muhammad al Baqir — Ja'far as Sadiq

Mu'awiya successfully claimed control over the Muslim Empire. As the 6th caliph he introduced the **Umayyad Dynasty** with its capital at **Damascus**. **Hassan** was poisoned to death soon after that.

When **Mu'awiya's** son, **Yazid**, took over the Caliphate after his father's death, Ali's younger son, **Husayn**, tried to lead an insurrection but could not rally enough support. Husayn's tragic death at the hands of the troops of Mu'awiya's son at the **Battle of Kerbala** in 680 was to become the paradigmatic event of Shi'a history.

---

9 According to some sources, when it looked as if Ali was going to win the war, Mu'awiya ordered his soldiers to hang pages of the Qur'an on the end of their spears to make Ali pause. The trick succeeded in forcing Ali to begin negotiations.

SPREAD OF ISLAM

UMYYAD DYNASTY (661-750)

The **Umayyad dynasty** centered in Damascus, Syria was introduced when **Mu'awiya**, the governor of Syria, succeeded **Ali** and his son, **Hassan**, as Muhammed's fifth successor (*caliph*). Under the Umayyads, the territories won by Islamic conquests developed into an Arab empire extending from North Africa and Spain to modern-day Uzbekistan in the east. In the new Muslim realm, Arabic became the official state language, coins were introduced and Christians and Jews ("People of the Book" or *dhimmies* who were allowed to practice their faith) were required to pay a poll tax (*jizya*).[10]

Hundreds of books were written and translated under the Umayyads and the major traditions of Islamic law began to be established. It was at this time, moreover, that the famous **Dome of the Rock** was built in Jerusalem over the spot where Muhammed was believed to have taken his "**Night Journey**" to the seven heavens. The **Al-Aqsa** (or "farthest") **Mosque** was built nearby to give Muslim pilgrims a place to worship.[11]

However, the Umayyad rulers were considered too secular and indulgent by conservative Muslims and too monarchical by the **Kharijites** and **Shi'as** who still saw them as usurpers.[12] After a revolt by a group of Syrian soldiers and a rebellion by Shi'as living in present-day Iran, the last Umayyad caliph and his family were killed[13] and the position of Caliph was filled by a descendent of Muhammed's uncle **Abbas,** an early supporter of the Prophet.

ABBASID DYNASTY (750-1258)

The more religious and cosmopolitan **Abbasids** launched Islam's Golden Age from their capital in Baghdad which became the most impressive city in the world (sometimes called "the Paris of the ninth century"). The city was filled with magnificent gardens, mosques and palaces that underscored the esteemed role of the *caliphs* who now considered themselves not only the successor to the Prophet but deputies of Allah himself.

---

[10] Jews and Christians, as "People of the Book," were accorded special status under the Muslim empire. As *dhimmies*, they were allowed to freely practice their own religions and manage their own communities but were prohibited from bearing arms, serving in public office or building religious structures taller than mosques.

[11] Both of the structures were built atop the **Noble Sanctuary**, the site of the Hebrew Temple in Jerusalem and the holiest spot on earth to the Jews, making the area the most contentious piece of real estate in the world.

[12] The Umayyads were a wealthy clan in Mecca that had opposed Muhammed and his followers. Because of this, they were also seen as outsiders.

[13] One member of the Umayyad family was able to escape and made his way to Spain where he established three centuries of Umayyad rule over al-Andalus (Spain) with the capital at Cordoba. Muslim or "Moorish" culture flourished in Spain and was dramatically different from the Iranian-Semitic culture that developed around the Abbasid Caliphate.

Under the Dynasty's greatest *caliphs*, **Harun al-Rashid** (famous because of his portrayal in the novel <u>A Thousand and One Nights</u>) and his son **al-Mamun**, great strides were made in mathematics, astronomy, chemistry, technology, medicine, literature and the Muslim religion. The mathematical system of algebra was developed at this time as were Arabic numerals (including a symbol for zero), and pharmaceutical remedies that are still used today. It was in this period that Abbasid Islamic scholars meticulously gathered details about the Prophet and his life and codified them in the form of **Hadith** (see chapter <u>Islamic Texts</u>).

But the empire began to decline after the appointment of **Mamun's** son as caliph. Provinces began to fall into the hands of independent dynasties and rebellions by Persian peasants, African slaves and other groups destabilized the central authority.

In 1258, Baghdad and the Abbasid Dynasty were wiped out by the **Mongols,** who unleashed a reign of terror on the population, killing more than 60 million people in the areas that became Iran and Iraq.

In time, the Mongols converted to Islam and restored the mosques and schools that had been destroyed.

FATIMID DYNASTY

By the mid 9th century, a group of Shi'as from the **Ismaili branch** (See chapter <u>Sects and Offshoots</u>) developed in Iraq with great ambitions to replace what they considered the illegitimate rule of the Abbasids.

By the early 10th century, these zealous Shi'a missionaries, who called themselves **Fatimids** after Fatima, Muhammed's daughter and the wife of Ali, the fourth caliph, spread their religion to Yemen and large sections of Egypt.

By 966, the Fatimids had successfully occupied Palestine and three years later conquered Egypt, where they founded a new capital that they called **Cairo**. After the Fatimids opened the famous **al-Azhar** university in 970, Egypt became the religious and intellectual center of the Muslim world. Despite their successes, the Fatimids faced much opposition from the Sunni Muslims and other Shi'a sects, especially when some of the Fatimid caliphs declared themselves the earthly incarnations of God.

Most destructive to the Fatimids' image, though, was the rule of the caliph **al-Hakim**, a capricious despot who made it a crime to sleep at night and work during the day, banned the making of women's shoes, ordered all dogs killed, forbade women from weeping at funerals and ordered Christians and Jews to wear crosses and bells. His persecution of Christian officials and especially the destruction of the Church of the Holy Sepulchre became the pretexts for the first Christian **Crusade** decades later. One evening, **al-**

Hakim mysteriously disappeared (the **Druze** [see chapter <u>Sects and Offshoots</u>] who still worship the Fatimid caliph, say he was spirited to heaven) and the **Fatimid** Empire continued to rule for another 150 years until it was invaded by the **Seljuk Turks**, a band of Sunni warriors from Turkistan in Central Asia.

SELJUK TURKS

The Sunni Muslim descendants of a tribal chief named **Seljuk** (the predecessors of the Ottoman Turks) had been employed as mercenaries by the Abbasids before they became a military force in their own right. Under the leadership of Seljuk's grandson, **Tughrol Beg**, who proclaimed himself Sultan in 1055, and his successor **Alp Ar Salan**, the Seljuks conquered Georgia, Armenia and much of Asia Minor. In 1070, they seized Syria and the holy cities of Palestine from the Fatimids and defeated the Byzantine Empire at **Manzikert**, a few miles from the Empire's capital (present-day Istanbul) the next year.

This invasion (along with concerns about the treatment of Christian pilgrims in Jerusalem) triggered the first Christian Crusade in 1095.

CRUSADES (1095 to 1270)

By the end of the 10th century, the Muslim world was split into three realms with each ruler claiming to be the **Caliph**. In the west, an **Umayyad** prince who had survived the destruction of his family's empire, set up his own Umayyad Empire, centered in Cordoba Spain (al-Andalus or Andalusia). In the east, the truncated **Abbasid** Dynasty ruled from Baghdad, and the **Fatimids** had established their own center of power in Cairo and ruled over Syria and Palestine.

A century later, the **Seljuks** seized Palestine and Syria from the Fatimids and were threatening the **Byzantine Empire** from Anatolia (present-day Turkey).

In Europe, meanwhile, the population was restive and the heads of the Christian Church were competing over claims to authority over the Christian community.

All these worlds collided at the beginning of the 11th century, when the Byzantine king asked **Pope Urban II** of the western Catholic Church for help in repelling the Muslim **Seljuk Turks,** who were massing on their border.

Hoping to assert the power of the Catholic Church and redirect local hostilities against an external enemy, the Pope decided to call on his subjects to reclaim the Holy Land from the "Muslim infidels." From 1095, waves of Crusaders were dispatched to Jerusalem, where they slaughtered the city's Muslim occupants and built Christian shrines over Muslim mosques.

AYYUBID DYNASTY

In Eygpt, meanwhile, the last Fatimid caliph had died (in 1171) and was replaced by a Sunni Kurd, **Saladin (Salah al Din al Ayyubi)**. Unlike his Shiite predecessors, Saladin was more interested in defending the Islamic culture from dissident Muslim sects and Christian European invaders than just protecting the territory. He wanted Cairo to be the center of an orthodox revival and built a number of prestigious *madrassas* (religious schools) to advance the religion.

In 1174, Saladin expanded his power base to Syria and 13 years later, recaptured Jerusalem from the Christian crusaders at the Battle of the **Horns of Hittin**.

Saladin is still considered one of Islam's greatest heroes because of his courage, humility and piety and has been portrayed in a number of European novels as the model chivalrous knight. But his **Ayyubid** Dynasty and Muslim control over Palestine didn't last long after his death in 1193.

By 1203, a fourth Crusade had begun which resulted in the capture of the Christian city of Constantinople by the Crusaders.

The **Mamelukes** took control over the **Ayyubid** dynasty in 1250.

MAMELUKES

Saladin and his **Ayyubid** successors imported Turkic slaves to Egypt from the Black Sea region to serve as mercenary soldiers. After they were trained as cavalry soldiers and had converted to Islam, these slaves (or **Mamelukes**, which translates as "owned") were given considerable freedom under the Ayyubid overlords and were even permitted to advance to positions of power and influence.

By 1250, the Mamelukes had become powerful enough to overthrow their masters as the Seljuk Turks had done centuries earlier. After the death of the last Ayyubid sultan in 1249 and the assassination of his heir, a Mameluke general married the Sultan's widow ushering in three hundred years of Mameluke rule.

MONGOLS

In 1215, a confederation of nomadic Mongolian tribes under the leadership of **Ghengis Khan** advanced from east of the Muslim lands sweeping through Turkistan, Iran, Afghanistan, the Caucasus and Russia, marauding and pillaging mercilessly before the Khan's death in 1227. Under Ghengis' grandson, **Hulagu Khan**, the horde of Mongols invaded Baghdad and, in 1258, the Mongols destroyed the city and murdered the Caliph (formally ending the Abbasid Caliphate). After killing the Caliph and 100s of 1000s of his subjects, the barbarians proceeded to destroy the Abbasids' vast irrigation system and the Empire's public works, including its magnificent libraries.

From Baghdad, the Mongol hordes made their way to Syria, leaving a trail of fires and destruction behind them.

They were finally stopped in 1260 in Palestine by the Mamelukes, who were then free to rule the Middle East unopposed until the rise of the Ottomans in the 16th century.

OTTOMAN EMPIRE[14]
In the wake of the Mongol's sweep from Asia to Palestine, another Muslim Dynasty emerged that would rule the territories surrounding the eastern half of the Mediterranean Sea until the 20th century.

The empire began as a small confederation of Turkish tribes who had migrated to Anatolia (present-day Turkey) to escape the Mongol invasion. Gathered in northwest Anatolia around a minor chieftain called **Osman**, these Muslim warriors were dedicated to the fight to capture land for Islam and were eager to expand their territory into the Roman Byzantine Empire across the border. In 1326, the **Osmanli** (or **Ottomans**) enjoyed their first victory by capturing the Byzantine town of Bursa.

By the end of the 14th century, the Ottomans had conquered Bulgaria, Macedonia and Serbia and were well on their way to capturing the Byzantine capital of Constantinople.

When Constantinople finally fell to the invaders in 1453, the Ottomans renamed it **Istanbul** and rebuilt the devastated city into a fabulously wealthy Muslim center. The city's capture not only brought an end to the Roman Byzantine Empire, but made the Ottomans the new masters of the Muslim Empire for the next 500 years.

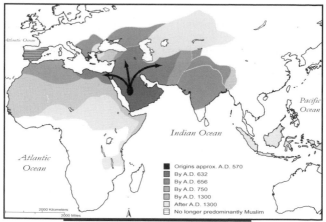

[14] For more on the Ottoman Empire, please see Roraback, Israel-Palestine in a Nutshell, Enisen Publishing, 2004

SUNNI/SHI'A SCHISM

Ten years after the migration or *hijrah*, the Prophet took his followers on one last pilgrimage to Mecca. On his way back, Shi'as claim, he gathered the Muslims around him in the village of **Ghadir Khumm** and announced "For whoever I am his leader, Ali is his leader." Soon after the declaration, Muhammed was on his deathbed.

Upon the Prophet's death, a meeting (*shura*) was held to decide who would succeed Muhammed as leader of the *ummah* (Muslim community). In disregard of Muhammed's earlier decision (at least according to Shi'as) the companions elected Muhammed's friend and supporter, the elder **Abu Bakr**, over his 30-year-old cousin and son-in-law, **Ali**. In the interest of peace and unity, Ali conceded.

In the course of his term as **Caliph**, Abu Bakr named **Umar bin Al Kattab** to be his successor. After Abu Bakr's death -- two years after becoming Caliph -- the appointment of **Umar** was confirmed by the elders, who appointed him the second Caliph, once again overlooking Ali.

Upon **Umar's** death, Ali was offered the position under the condition that he abide by the precedents set by **Abu Bakr** and **Umar**. When Ali refused, the Caliphate was awarded to **Uthman ibn Affan**.

After **Uthman's** assassination in 656, Ali was finally selected to be the Muslim community's fourth caliph. Ali and his followers, who finally felt vindicated, had little time to celebrate. **Uthman's** relatives (under their patriarch, the Syrian governor **Mu'awiya**) and two of **Uthman's** former companions (who had been joined by **Aisha**, one of Muhammed's wives) rebelled against the fourth caliph because of his hesitance to bring Uthman's killers to justice.[15].

When Ali, himself, was assassinated by a Kharijite, his oldest son, **Hassan**, briefly became caliph until he was forced to abdicate by threat of force by **Mu'awiaya,** who then assumed the position. Mu'awiya's son, **Yazid**, took over the Caliphate after his father's death.

When **Husayn** (Ali's second son by **Fatima**, Muhammed's daughter), battled to retake the Caliphate from **Yazid**, he, too, was murdered at the **Battle of Kerbala** (in Iraq) in 680.

SHI'AS

From the moment **Abu Bakr** was chosen to lead the Muslim community instead of Ali in A.D. 632, a small band of believers split from the rest. The **Shi'as** (short for *shi'at Ali* or "party of Ali" in Arabic) believed that Muhammed had explicitly designated Ali as his successor as evidenced in a

---

[15] In such a period of turmoil, explain Shi'as, Ali was fearful that he might condemn the wrong man. His hesitation in convicting Uthman, therefore, was driven by his desire to conduct proper justice.

statement they claim the Prophet had made that "Ali is my brother, my executor and my successor among you." To the Shi'as, furthermore, only the "People of the House," or members of the Prophet's family, had the legitimate right to rule; hence the first three caliphs had usurped Ali's rightful position as leader of the *umma* (the Muslim community).

Shi'as believe that, along with his birthright, Ali had a special spiritual function alongside the Prophet that gave him a preeminent right to lead the faithful. Shi'as, therefore, negated the Caliphate and have always revered Ali as the first legitimate leader (**Imam**) of the Muslims with the position being passed on to his descendants

The Imams, according to Shi'as, possessed spiritual powers and unique gifts. As "infallible vessels of God's light," (passed down from the prophets to the Imams) they were endowed with the ability and responsibility to serve as intercessors between men and God, according to members of the largest branch of Shi'as, the **Twelvers**.

THE MARTYRDOM OF HUSAYN
The A.D. 680 martyrdom of Ali's son, **Husayn**, at the massacre at **Kerbala** is the cornerstone event for the Shi'as, who yearly commemorate his bravery and sacrifice in mourning rituals and sympathetic self-injury (during the **Ashura**). Themes of guilt, suffering, betrayal and public atonement permeate the Shi'a community, who also believe that their Imams had been poisoned by the Caliphs.

DIFFERENT PRACTICES
Along with the commemoration of the martyrdom of Muhammed's descendants (unique to the sect), the Shi'as observe some of their own specific laws and customs. They reject the Hadith that had been collected by the Sunnis (those who follow the Prophet's example or *sunna*), believing that anyone who had not acknowledged Ali's preeminence as leader of the Muslim community had no legitimate right to pass on the words and deeds of Muhammed.

In place of the Sunni-accepted Hadith, Shi'as compiled their own accounts of the Prophets life and words and observed a slightly different interpretation of the **Qur'an**.

Although Shi'as abide by the **Five Pillars** (see chapter Five Pillars of Islam) as do their Sunni counterparts, the Shi'as pray only three times a day (by performing the afternoon prayer immediately after the noon prayer, and the nighttime prayer after the sunset prayer). Twelver Shi'as accept temporary marriages. The Shi'as also consider a visit to the grave sites of the Shia martyrs as an important act (although not as important as the pilgrimage to Mecca, the *Hajj*).

Twelver Shi'as also believe that a savior, a **Mahdi** (the last of the Imams)

will establish a divine kingdom of justice on earth. Until then, the Imam will remain hidden (see chapter Sects and Offshoots)

IMAMATE

While the Sunnis believed any qualified adult male could follow the Prophet's leadership, the Shi'as claimed that Ali and his male descendants had a secret prophetic knowledge that was passed down from father to son and so constituted the true succession. Having survived the **Battle of Kerbala** which he fought with his father, **Husayn's** son **Zayn al-Abidin** was thereby deemed the 4th Imam.

The succession passed down to his son, **Muhammed al-Baqir** and grandson, **Ja'far as-Sadiq**, who were recognized by most Shi'as as legitimate rulers. From there, however, the line split. (See "List of Imams" in Sects and Offshoots).

TWELVERS

By far the largest branch of Shi'ism (with over 80 million adherents), the **Twelvers** followed Ali's line of successors to **Muhammed al-Mahdi** who, they claim, had disappeared in 873 and has remained hidden ever since. While he is in hiding, though, the "hidden Imam" continues to guide religious scholars who have been chosen to preside over the Shi'a Islamic community until he returns on Judgment Day. The late **Ayatollah Khomeini**, who led the Iranian Revolution in 1978, was considered by a few Shi'as as Islam's temporal leader.

Twelvers today make up about 60% of the population of Iraq and Twelver Shi'ism became (and still is) the official religion of Iran (Persia) when the **Safavids** came to power in 1501.

SEVENERS (Ismailis)

The Seveners claimed **Ishmail** (who had died before his father, **Ja'far as-Sadiq**, the 6th Imam) was the last Imam thereby completing a full circle of history. The most complex and magical sect, the Seveners opted to hide the identity of their spiritual leaders and infused the religion with elements derived from Platonic philosophy, astrology, Hermetic sciences and other diverse beliefs. From the Ishmaili sect arose a number of offshoots including the **Assassins** (Arabic hashishiyun or "hashish eaters") who used political assassination as a means for furthering their power.

FIVERS (Zaydites or Zaydis)

The Fivers (established in Yemen) considered **Zayd**, the son of the 4th Imam, who had died fighting against the Umayyads in 740, as the last rightful Imam. From then on all the leaders were elected from among Ali's descendants. The Fivers have become the most moderate of all Shi'a groups and the closest to the Sunnis.

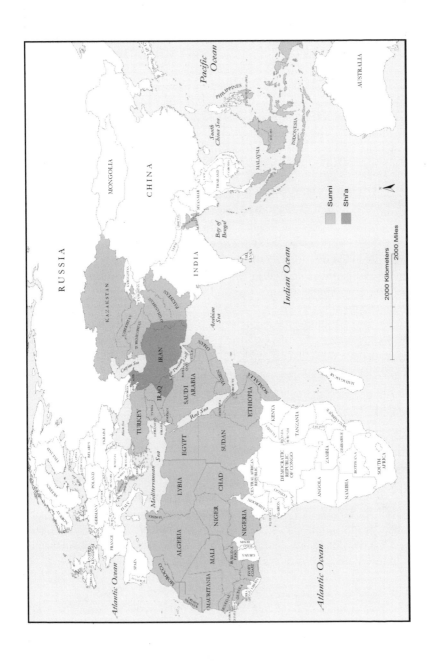

FIVE PILLARS OF ISLAM

While the recognized legitimate line of successor, the style of dress and Islamic structural preferences may differ among various Muslim sects, all believers are bound unequivocally by the following five fundamental pillars (requirements).

AFFIRMATION (Shahada)

Recitation of the basic statement of the Islamic faith:

"There is no God but God (Allah) and Muhammed is his messenger"

Anyone who sincerely repeats this statement three times aloud in front of a witness is considered a Muslim. Conversely anyone who cannot wholeheartedly recite this statement is not a Muslim.

A Muslim may fail to observe the other pillars of the Muslim religion (prayer, alms, fasting, and pilgrimage) but will always be considered an adherent as long as he observes the Shahadah.

PRAYERS (Salah or Salat)

A Muslim is required to pray towards Mecca (*qibla*) five times a day as long as he or she is physically able. The first prayer of the day is performed between dawn and sunrise, the second when the sun is at its zenith, the third in the afternoon, the fourth at sundown and the

---

GOD HAS NINETY-NINE NAMES

There are 2,700 references to God in the Qur'an but it is his 99 names (or Attributes) that are most honored by Muslims. Muslims believe that committing these names to memory is very important.

In the opening statement of the Qur'an, called the **Basmalla**, God is praised for two of his qualities, *Bismallah al-Rahman al-Rahim* or "God the Merciful, the Compassionate." Other names include, God the King (Al-Malik), the Most Holy (Al-Quddus), the Almighty (Al-Aziz), the Creator (Al-Khaliq), the Bestower (Al-Wahhab), the Victory-Giver (Al-Fattah), the Magnificent (Al-Azim), the Wise (Al-Hakim), the All-Glorious (Al-Majid), the All-Praiseworthy (Al-Hamid), The All-Inclusive (Al-Wahid), The Inheritor of All (Al-Warith), the Guide (Al-Rashid).

Muslims may add the qualification "Abd" (or "servant of") before one of God's attributes in their names. Thus the name of the first monarch of Saudi Arabia, **Abdul Aziz bin Abdul Rahman ibn Faisal Al Saud** translates as "Servant of God the Almighty, Son of the Servant of God the Merciful, Son of Faisal of Saud."

---

last prayer of the day is performed in the evening before going to bed. In this way, a Muslim is obliged to honor his faith at all times, even during the hustle and bustle of the day. Shi'a Muslims combine two of the prayers requiring them to pray only three times in the day.

In order for the prayer to be valid, the religious observer and the immediate surroundings must be clean. Before praying, therefore, Muslims prepare themselves by washing their faces, hands, arms, feet, ears etc. and, if they are praying at home, must keep the prayer area spotless.[16] If there is no water available, as might have been the case in the arid deserts of Arabia, Muslims are permitted to use a pebble or a fistful of sand to symbolically clean the body of impurities. In another gesture of cleanliness, most devotees prostrate themselves on a specially designated prayer rug.

Both sexes are separated during the prayer service. Women who choose to attend the mosque for *salah* usually gather at the back of the room and pray behind curtains or blinds. It's considered improper for a man to witness a woman bent over in reverent prostration.

ALMS (Zakah or Zakat)

All Muslims are obliged to give alms to the poor on a stipulated scale. The amount of the "religious tax" is determined by calculating a percentage of a person's possessions, capital and income. A voluntary donation is also encouraged as long as it is done discreetly.

FASTING (Sawm)

Beginning at the first crescent moon in the month of **Ramadan** (when Muhammed received his first revelation from God) each Muslim must abstain from eating, drinking, smoking or having sexual relations between sun-up and sun-down. The ritual fast is intended to help believers master self-restraint and to share the distress of the underprivileged.

Pregnant and nursing mothers are exempt from the duty, as are travelers, the sick, young children and women who are menstruating. However, any missed fasting days must be made up at a later date.

PILGRIMMAGE (Hajj)

Once in a lifetime, the physically fit and financially able Muslim must make a pilgrimage to Mecca, Saudi Arabia. As in the days of Muhammed, the believer performs a series of elaborate rites at the site of the Ka'aba at a particular time of year as set forth in the Islamic calendar.

Each year, millions of Muslims simultaneously gather in Mecca to walk seven times around the sacred structure (the **Ka'aba**) in imitation of the angels who circumambulate the heavenly throne. All the pilgrims then run between two hills in memory of Hagar's panic to find water for her son, Ishmael, and sacrifice animals in homage to Abraham's near sacrifice of his son to God. After a day of meditation, the Muslims then throw pebbles at

---

[16] The Ablution (or cleansing) is symbolic of baptism.

stone slabs symbolizing Satan and finally sanctify themselves by sacrificing all or part of their hair. Many Muslims shave their heads completely, women generally remove only a lock of hair.

More than simply a profound spiritual experience for the Muslims, the pilgrimage also brings the community together in intense recognition of the unity of the faithful and offers the opportunity to strengthen the Muslim identity. (**Malcolm X** abandoned the Nation of Islam's racist bias against whites after his spiritual pilgrimage [see chapter Sects and Offshoots).

Around two million Muslims carry out the *hajj* each year. Those who complete the requirement may add the title "Hajji" (or "pilgrim") before their names.

JIHAD

The concept of "jihad" in Islam is so important that it is often considered the "sixth pillar." But despite popular misconception, the word simply means "struggle" or "striving" and can be applied to all things one must strive for or against. The struggle against one's own vices, for instance, is considered a *jihad* as well as a struggle against those things that threatened the Islamic faith.

A defensive military jihad – considered the "lesser" of the two types of jihad – is a very serious duty and must follow strict guidelines in order to be considered legitimate.

A true defensive Islamic jihad should not target other Muslims, unless the warriors are fighting for liberation from tyranny. Women, children, the elderly and the infirm should not be harmed and prisoners should be treated humanely.

ISLAMIC TEXTS

QUR'AN

One evening while the Prophet Muhammed meditated under the night sky in Mecca, in present-day Saudi Arabia, he received a message from God sent through the angel **Gabriel**. On that night in A.D. 610 (still commemorated yearly during the holy month of **Ramadan**), the Prophet learned that he had been chosen to receive the word of God. Throughout the next two decades, he would receive a number of divine communications from Allah that would eventually be compiled into what Muslims say is the final holy book, the **Koran** (or Koran).

Muslims believe that the sheer magnificence of the book (its poetic prose, its numerical composition) is a testament to Muhammed's divine status in the same way that Jesus miraculously healed the sick and Moses parted the Red Sea. The phenomenon is even more significant when one considers the fact that the Prophet could not read or write. The revelations he received were verbally recounted to his followers who were instructed to memorize and recite passages (*sura*) on a regular basis in order to ensure that the meaning remained pure and complete. [17]

Nineteen years after Muhammed's death, **Uthman ibn Affan**, the third Caliph, gathered all the records of what was believed to be God's literal words and compiled them into the holy **Qur'an**. Although the chronology of the revelations was lost in the process (the 114 chapters or *suras* were organized by length, beginning with the longest chapter and ending with the shortest, rather than in the order in which the verses were received), the book is considered by Muslims to be the most accurate account of God's message in existence today.[18] In contrast, Muslims claim, portions of the Jewish and Christian scriptures (from which many of the lessons and narratives in the Qur'an have been drawn), have been corrupted or altered by scribes, religious leaders or translators years after they were originally presented to the prophets.

The text was written and continues to be read in the same language in which it was conferred to the prophet. In order to fully appreciate the true message of the holy Qur'an and to preserve the religion in its purist form, Muslims are encouraged to read, recite and memorize the book in its original Arabic.

THE BIBLE AND THE QUR'AN

The Muslims hold the belief that throughout history, God sent revelations to earth a number of times to prophets who compiled them into holy books. By the seventh century, though, many of the books had been lost or altered

---

[17] The literal translation of the word "Qur'an" or "Koran" is "recitation" or "reading."

[18] 15:9 *We have, without doubt, sent down the message, and we will assuredly guard it from corruption.*

through translations, interpretations and other modifications. Although the **Tanach** (or Old Testament) and the **New Testament** of the **Bible** are believed to have been originally divinely inspired and therefore worthy of respect,[19] parts of them are considered by Muslims as unreliable sources of God's true will.

The Qur'an, it is believed, was transmitted by God through the angel Gabriel to Muhammed in order to refine the message that had been sent earlier (through Moses, Jesus etc.). For this reason, many of the narratives in the Qur'an are similar to those found in the Judeao-Christian scriptures.

CREATION

Bible: According to the Biblical Book of Genesis, God created the earth in six days. On the first day, he created light; on the second day, he created the sky; on the third day he created the earth, the sea and plants; the fourth day, he separated day from night by creating the sun, the moon and the stars; on the fifth day he created fish and birds and on the sixth day he created animals and human beings. By the seventh day, God had finished his work and (according to passages in Exodus) he rested.

Qur'an: The Qur'an also says that God created the earth in six days in roughly the same successive stages (although the narration is scattered in passages all over the Book). But creation was only the prelude. On the seventh day, God did not rest but was then "firmly established on the throne of authority" (Qur'an verses [*suras*] 7:54 and 32:5)

ADAM AND EVE

Bible: After he created the heavens and the earth, God created **Adam** out of soil on the ground and breathed into his nostrils to give him life. He then put Adam into the Garden of Eden and warned him that he could eat from any tree he liked except the **Tree of Knowledge,** which would cause him to die.

Later, God decided that Adam needed a companion and put him into a deep sleep. When he awoke he found that God had created a woman from one of his ribs.

Adam and his new mate **Eve** lived peacefully in the **Garden of Eden** until Eve was tempted by a snake, the "most cunning animal that the Lord had made," who told her that eating from the fobidden fruit would give her the wisdom to know the difference between good and evil but would not kill her. So she ate the fruit and gave some to her husband.

---

[19] Muslims are encouraged to become familiar with the Jewish and Christian scriptures.

Qur'an: After he created the heavens and the earth, God created man first out of potter's clay, then out of sperm-drop and then into a leech-like clot. When the elements were mixed and formed into a human being, God breathed his spirit into him.

In the Qur'an, God created man and woman from a single person (**Eve**'s name is never mentioned, nor does it specify whether or not she came from **Adam's** rib) and made them of like nature. He put both of his creations in the **Garden of Eden** (or Paradise) and warned them not to eat from a certain tree in the garden.

But acting on whispered suggestions from Satan, both Adam and his mate disobeyed God and tasted the fruit of the forbidden tree in hopes that they would become angels and live forever. Instead, they became aware of their nakedness and God punished them for their defiance by casting them out of Eden to live on earth until the Day of Judgment. (In the Bible women are collectively punished through pain in childbirth and men are doomed to live a life of toil).

In the Qur'an, both Adam and his companion are tempted by Satan and both are held equally responsible for their sin. Also in contrast to the Bible (which infuses the event with the concept of "Original Sin") God later forgives the first man and woman for their disobedience (though they are never let back into the Garden of Paradise).

It is also believed that Adam was the original founder of the Ka'bah, the structure built around the sacred stone in Mecca, Saudi Arabia, as a sanctuary consecrated to God. After Adam's death, tradition says that the Ka'bah was rebuilt by his son Seth and again, over time, by the descendants of Noah.

NOAH

Both the Bible and the Qur'an tell us that God instructed Noah to build an Ark to save his family and two of every species on earth from a great flood. In the Bible, though, Noah is joined by his three sons (**Shem, Ham** and **Japheth**) while the Qur'an says that one of his sons refused to board the boat and drowned. In the Qur'an, moreover, it is claimed that the Ark came to rest on **Mount Judi.** In the Bible it lands on **Mount Ararat** (both are in southern Turkey).

ABRAHAM

Bible: According to the book of Genesis in the Bible, **Abram** (later "Abraham"), a descendent of Noah's son **Shem**, lived in the city of **Ur** in Babylonia (present-day Iraq) with his barren wife **Sarai** (later known as "Sarah"). When God promised Abram that his descendants would become a great nation if he left his native land, Abram, his wife Sarai and his nephew **Lot** set out to settle in the land of **Canaan** (the land that God promised would belong to him and his descendants). In Canaan Abram built an altar to the Lord (the future Temple Mount in Jerusalem).

In order to fulfill God's promise that Abram's progeny would inherit the lands from the border of Egypt to the Euphrates River, his wife (who could not have children of her own) offered him her Egyptian slave girl named **Hagar**.

When Hagar became pregnant with Abram's child, Sarai became jealous and treated her slave so cruelly that she ran away. While she walked in the desert, though, an angel promised Hagar that if she returned to her mistress, she would have so many descendants that no one would be able to count them.

She returned as instructed and bore Abram a son called **Ishmael**. Four years later, Abram was given the name "Abraham" because he would become the ancestor of many nations (the name in Hebrew sounds like the word for "ancestor of many nations.")

To seal God's covenant, Abraham agreed that every baby born to his people would be circumcised when he was eight days old. As a reward for his loyalty, God gave Sarah (who had been barren and no longer of childbearing age) the ability to bear a child who would be named **Isaac**.

One day Sarah saw Ishmael, the son of her slave girl, playing with Isaac and, fearing that Ishmael would receive some of the inheritance that belonged to Isaac, sent Hagar into the wilderness of Paran (some Muslims contend that "Paran" is an ancient name for "Mecca" in present-day Saudi Arabia).

According to the Bible, some time later, God tested Abraham by commanding him to offer his son Isaac as a sacrifice. Moments before Abraham was about to commit the fatal act, God stopped him and sent a ram to be used as a burnt-offering in his place.

Qur'an: The Qur'an provides a more detailed description of Abraham in his youth as the son of an idolater (one who worships many idols). In one story, Abraham, believing in the sole power of God's divinity, becomes upset with the local practice of worshipping stone idols that they themselves constructed. To show the townspeople how misguided they have become, Abraham broke all but the largest idol into pieces while the people were celebrating elsewhere. When they returned they were enraged by his actions. In defense, Abraham claimed that it was not he, but the largest idol that was responsible for the destruc-

tion. If they didn't believe him, he said, they could ask the idols themselves. When they admitted that the idols could not speak, Abraham chided the idolaters for worshipping powerless

> Muslims claim that Abraham was the first person to bow to the will of Allah in submission (or "Islam") making him the first official Muslim ("he who submits").

objects that they had created rather than the God who had created human beings.

The people of Ur were enraged and threw Abraham in a blazing fire. God helped him escape from the fire and, with his nephew Lot, Abraham went to the land promised by God to him and his descendants.

Like the Jews and Christians, Muslims believe that Abraham had a son with his wife's servant Hagar (*Hajarah*) called Ishmael (*Ismail*) and that the two were cast out into the desert because of Sarah's jealousy. When their water ran out, Hagar ran between two hills in anguish until water sprang beneath her feet (from the well of **Zam Zam**). Muslims maintain that Hagar and Ishmael settled in Mecca where Ishmael became the father of the Northern Arabians.

Although the Qur'an acknowledges the importance of Isaac as a righteous prophet of God, Muslims believe that his miraculous birth to Sarah was a reward given to Abraham for preparing to sacrifice his first-son Ishmael.

37:102 "Then when the son reached that age of serious work with him, he said: 'O my son! I see in vision that I offer thee in sacrifice. Now see what is they view!' The son said: 'O my father! Do as thou art commanded: thou will find me, if God so wills, one practicing patience and constancy!"

Although Ishmael's name isn't expressly stated, Muslims conclude that for the first 14 years of Ishmael's life, he was Abraham's only son and therefore, the "son" in question. In the Qur'an, moreover, the son consents to the sacrifice whereas in the Bible, Isaac asks "where is the lamb for sacrifice?" to which Abraham responds "God will provide it."

Once the two had submitted their wills to God (*islam*) and Ishmael was about to receive the fatal blow, God determined that they had satisfactorily acted out the vision and rewarded them.[20]

Tradition holds that during a visit, Abraham and his first-born son **Ishmael** rebuilt the **Ka'bah**, (a large cubic stone structure surrounding the sacred Black Stone revered by Muslims) replacing a temple that had first been erected by Adam. Many of the rituals performed during the **Hajj** (the mandatory visit to Mecca – see chapter titled <u>Pillars of Islam</u>) recount the trials of Hagar and Ishmael and the involvement of Abraham. (For instance, pilgrims perform prayers at the station of Abraham, reenact Hagar's frantic search for water and then drink from the **Zam Zam Well**).

MOSES

Bible: The story of Moses is told in both the **Torah** (Old Testament) and the **Gospels** (New Testament) beginning with his birth at a time when the Pharaoh of Egypt had commanded that all male children born to Hebrews should be killed. To save her child, **Jochebed** put her baby in a makeshift boat and sent him adrift on the Nile River. The baby was found by **Pharaoh's** daughter who adopted him as her son and named him "Moses."

As an adult, Moses went to see his fellow Hebrews and killed an Egyptian who had been taunting one of the Hebrew slaves. After the crime was discovered, Moses escaped his death sentence by fleeing to the desert where he worked as a shepherd for his father-in-law, Jethro. It was here in the desert that Moses came in contact with God in the form of a burning bush. From the middle of the bush, God spoke to him revealing his name, and telling Moses to return to Egypt and rescue his people from their bondage in Egypt.

With the help of his elder brother **Aaron**, Moses persuaded the Pharaoh to let his people go. His demand was accompanied by ten plagues that God had sent to terrorize the Egyptians. On their journey back to the **Promised Land (Israel)** in the land of Canaan, God presented Moses with the **Ten Commandments** written on two tablets.

After 40 years, the Hebrews finally return to Canaan.

Qur'an: The story of Moses is recounted almost in its entirety in the Qur'an with greater detail (for instance Muslims say that Moses had a speech impediment) and slight differences (the baby was found by Pharaoh's wife, not daughter). The Qur'an speaks about the burning

---

[20] Muslims celebrate Abraham's proffered sacrifice during the Festival of the Sacrifice or **Eid ul Adha**. This is the second official holiday after the Festival of the Fast Breaking [**Eid ul Fitr**] that ends the fast required during the holy month of Ramadan).

bush, the plagues, the parting of the Red Sea[21] and discusses at length Moses receiving of the Ten Commandments.

2:87 We [God] gave Moses the Book and followed him up with a succession of Apostles. (Jesus, Muhammed et al.) 6:154 We [God] gave Moses The Book, completing our favor to those who would do right, and explaining all things in detail, — and a guide and a mercy, that they might believe in the meeting with their Lord.

JESUS

Bible: In the Gospels (four books in the New Testament of the Christian Bible that recount Christ's life and teachings), Jesus is described as the son of Mary, a virgin at the time of his birth, and her fiancé Joseph (whose genealogical line is traced back fourteen generations from Abraham to David). It is explained that Jesus was conceived by the Holy Spirit in fulfillment of an earlier prophecy.

The Bible also teaches that Jesus is the son of God, God incarnate, as well as the promised Messiah (savior). In John 10:30, Jesus said "The Father and I are one."

According to the Gospels, Jesus was baptized by John the Baptist (known in the Qur'an as "Yahya"), he preached in Galilee, performed miracles and healed people afflicted with all kinds of illnesses.

Jesus' powerful influence and popularity threatened the authority of the chief priests of Israel who ordered him arrested for what they believed was a blasphemous claim that he was the promised Messiah and the King of the Jews. Under pressure from the priests and a Jewish mob, the Roman Governor, Pontius Pilate, handed Jesus over to be crucified.

After a woeful march through Jerusalem, Jesus was nailed to a cross until he died. At the moment of his death, "the earth shook, the rocks split apart, the graves broke open and many of God's people who had died were raised to life." His body was wrapped in a linen sheet and placed in a tomb.

Three days later, says the Bible, Jesus rose from the dead and visited his disciples once again in Galilee.

---

[21] The Jews believed that the day after Moses was delivered from the Egyptians; he observed a fast in gratitude. A few Muslims also observe this act by fasting on the day called "**Ashura**." Although the date and name are more closely associated with the Shi'a holiday commemorating the death of Ali's grandson Husayn, some Sunni Hadith document Ashura as the day God accepted Adam's repentance after his exile from paradise, the day God saved Noah and his companions in the ark, the day Moses received the Ten Commandments, the day Jonas was taken out of the belly of a fish and other notable events.

Qur'an: Mary, the mother of Jesus is also revered in the Qur'an as the woman whom God (Allah) had "chosen above women of all nations" (3:42). Her importance is so great, in fact, that a Qur'anic chapter (*sura*) was named after the virgin mother of Jesus (chapter 19 called "Maryam"). While Mary's background and trials are described in greater detail than they are in the Bible (in order to explain why she had been chosen to be the mother of Jesus) no mention is made of her husband, Joseph.

In the Qur'an, the miracle of Jesus' birth from a virgin mother is further reinforced by accounts that the baby had the ability to speak from the cradle.

19:27 *"How can we talk to one who is a child in the cradle?" and Jesus said "I am indeed a servant of God. He hath given me Revelation and made me a prophet.*

Where the Bible and the Qur'an greatly differ is in Jesus' divine status. The biblical claim that Jesus is the son of God is fervently refuted in the Qur'an.

NAMES IN TRANSLATION
Bible - *Qur'an*
Aaron *(Harun)*
Abraham *(Ibrahim)*
David *(Dawud)*
Elias/Elijah *(Ilyas)*
Ezra *('Uzayr)*
Gabriel, Angel *(Jibril)*
God *(Allah)*
Isaac *(Ishaq)*
Ishmael *(Isma'il)*
Jacob *(Ya'qub)*
Jesus *(Isa)*
Job *(Ayyub)*
John the Baptist *(Yahya)*
Jonah *(Yunus)*
Joseph *(Yusuf)*
Lot *(Lut)*
Lucifer/Satan *(Iblis,Shaytaan)*
Mary *(Maryam)*
Moses *(Musa)*
Noah *(Nuh)*

4:171 *"Christ Jesus the son of Mary was no more than an apostle of God, and his word, which he bestowed on Mary, and a Spirit proceeding from him: so believe in God and His apostles. Say not "Trinity": desist: It will be better for you: For God is One God: Glory be to Him: Far exalted is He above having a son. To Him belong all things in the heavens and on earth. And enough is God as a disposer of affairs."*

Muslims also believe that Jesus never actually died. His death by crucifixion, they claim, was only an illusion. Rather, Jesus was raised up to God and will return to earth on Judgement Day to fight the anti-Christ.

4:157 *That they said in boast, 'We killed Christ Jesus, the son of Mary, the Apostle of God" – but they killed him not, nor crucified him, but so it was made to appear to them ...* 4:158 *Nay, God raised him up unto Himself ...*

HADITH (Traditions or Accounts)

Lest the words of God be confused with those of Muhammed himself, the Prophet initially forbade his followers to write down his personal sayings until the sanctity of the Qur'an was clearly established. When the prohibition was lifted, his companions meticulously took note of Muhammed's activities, his lessons, his instructions and his way of living.

Three hundred years after Muhammed's death, religious scholars began to compile information collected from the *Hadith* (or "conversations") passed down orally from generation to generation by those who had had contact with the Prophet. Reports and legends were gathered from all over the Muslim world and exhaustively analyzed for authenticity. The most famous collector, **Muhammed ibn Ismail al-Bukhari,** for instance, collected over 600,000 *Hadith* but included only 2,206 in his official book because he could not prove that the others were genuine.

Debates abound in the Muslim community over the authenticity of the various *Hadith*. Some of the most dependable *Hadith* (for example, the works of Bukhari and **Abdul Husayn Muslim**)[22] are observed while others are excluded by some Muslims. Other believers dismiss all the *Hadith* deeming them unreliable or (at worst) fabricated texts. The Shi'as, on the other hand, accept only the Hadith that can be traced back to the words of Ali or the Imams who succeeded him.

SUNNAH (lit. "Custom," the way of life of Mohammed)

While the *Hadith* are narrations about the life of the Prophet, the *Sunnah* (from which the word "Sunni" is derived) provides an account of what the Prophet actually said and how he lived including the things he allowed or condoned and the things he himself refrained from doing or disapproved of (the Qur'an is considered the word of God).

In addition to the "Five Pillars of Islam," pious Muslims are encouraged to model their actions after the customary practice of Muhammed – although the Sunnah also includes practices that only apply to the Prophet and are not permitted to his followers (for example, only Muhammed was allowed to have more than four wives).

---

[22] Four other collections of well-respected Hadith are Sunan of Tirmidhi, Nasa'i, Ibn Majah, and Abu Da'ud. Together with the works of Bukhari and Muslim, these books are called the "six books" or *"al-kutub al-sitta."*

ISLAMIC JURISPRUDENCE

A Muslim's religion is more than just a spiritual state -- it is a lifestyle. And nearly every aspect of a Muslim's existence, from the correct way to pray to the proper way to conduct business, can be drawn from guidelines set forth in the **Qur'an**, the **Hadith** and the **Sunnah.**

Over the course of centuries, the rules of proper Islamic conduct (or *fiqh*) have been codified in the form of four major Sunni schools of law (**Maliki, Hanafi, Shafii** and **Hanbali**) and by Shi'a laws of jurisprudence (called **Ja'fari**).

SUNNI SCHOOLS OF LAW

The four schools of Sunni Sharia Law agree on most of their rulings but differ in their interpretations of Qur'anic passages, the Hadith they accept as authentic and the weight they give to modern rulings determined by historical precedent or "analogies" (*qiyas*) and popular consensus (*ijma*)[23] when applying Islamic tenets to everyday life. Each of the schools also reflects the culture and era of the classical jurists (interpreters of Islamic law) that founded the movements – which accounts for some of their antiquated rulings.

MALIKI

Founder – **Malik ibn Anas** (died A.D. 795) (Born in Medina, present-day Saudi Arabia)
Dominant in North, West and Central Africa and parts of Egypt, Sudan and Morocco

The Maliki is the oldest of the four schools (or *madhhabs*) and the second-largest followed by approximately 25% of all Muslims. The school is different from the others since it draws not only on the Qur'an, and examples from the Sunnah and Hadith to determine correct Islamic practice, but also on the practices of the people of Medina since the Prophet and most of his companions lived there and his followers remained there after his death.

The law book of its founder, Malik, is the earliest known Muslim legal text.

---

[23] Applied to situations not dealt with in the other books – for example, regarding contemporary issues like abortion, organ donation, cryogenics etc.

HANAFI

Founder – Nu'man Abu Hanifah (died A.D. 767) (Born in Kufa in present-day Iraq)

Dominant in the Indian subcontinent (India and Pakistan), Afghanistan,[24] Iraq and most countries that were formerly part of the Turkish Ottoman Empire (Egypt, Turkey, the Levant [Israel, Palestine, Jordan, Syria]) – (Hanafis were appointed judges in the Ottoman Empire and hence were responsible for writing the authoritative code of law for public life and the administration of justice).

Branches: Barelvi and Deobandi

> The Hanafi School (followed by approximately 30% of Muslims worldwide and 85% of Sunni Muslims living in South Asia) is considered the most liberal school and the one most open to modern ideas. Its founder, **Hanafi**, accepted the Qur'an but rejected most of the Hadith. He believed that codes of conduct not found in the Qur'an should be determined by popular opinion (*ijma*) and analogy (*qiyas*) and should suit the local culture. The school, therefore, elevates the importance of belief over practice and is tolerant of differences within Muslim communities.

> Adherents also believe that the state should not interfere in the relationship between man and God (the school was opposed to the power of the caliphs).

> The Hanafi school is divided into two major groups, the Barelvi Hanafis and Deobandis.

> The **Barelvis** (mostly from the Pakistan province of Punjab) believe that the Prophet Muhammed has superhuman qualities and is present all around us at all times. They also believe in the intercession between God and humans through holy men called *pirs*.

> **Deobandis** (who inspired the fundamentalist **Taliban** movement[25]) believe that Islamic societies have fallen behind the West because they have been seduced by amoral and materialistic temptations of Westernization. The branch originally attracted Muslims who were hostile to British rule in India and its adherents were dedicated to the purification of Islam by ridding it of corrupt Western influences and reemphasizing the models of conduct established in the Qur'an and the Sunnah. Deobandis also believed that it was a sacred duty to go anywhere in the world to protect the Muslim community through *jihad*.

---

[24] The 2003 Afghan constitution (based on the 1964 constitution) stated that "religious rites performed by the state shall be according to the provisions of the Hanafi School of jurisprudence."

[25] Most members of the Taliban leadership attended Deobandi-influenced *madrassas* (religious schools) in Pakistan before coming to power in the 1990s.

SHAFII

Founder – Mohammad ibn Idris ash Shafii (died A.D. 820) (Born in Mecca, present-day Saudi Arabia) Shafii belonged to the Quraysh tribe and was a distant relative of the Prophet Muhammed.

Dominant in Indonesia, Thailand and the Philippines. It is the state religion of Brunei and Malaysia

The Shafi school (followed by approximately 15% of Muslims worldwide), is considered the easiest school of law to abide by in terms of social and personal rules (the Hanbali school is considered the hardest).

HANBALI

Founder: **Imam Ahmad ibn Hanbal** (died A.D. 855) (born in Baghdad, present-day Iraq)

Dominant only in Saudi Arabia and Qatar

Branches: Wahhabi

Ahmad ibn Hanbal, the founder of the Hanbali school, was known for his literal interpretation of the Qur'an, his outspoken prohibition of innovation and his extensive use of Hadith as a source of law over popular opinion and analogy. In fact his major contribution to Islamic scholarship was a collection of more than 30,000 Hadith known as **"Musnad Ahmad"** (or "Musnad Hanbal").

The Hanbali school is the least popular (fewer than 5% adherents)[26] and most conservative of the four schools. Its followers have been considered reactionary because of their fanatical intolerance of views different from their own and their habit of observing rigid rules of conduct.

In the 18th century, the Hanbali School was invigorated by the reformist movement of **Muhammed Ibn abd al-Wahhab,** the founder of **Wahhabism (Salafism)** that is practiced today in Saudi Arabia (see "Wahhabism" in <u>Sects and Off-shoots</u> chapter).

---

[26] Throughout history Hanbalis have suffered bouts of persecution against them because of their fanatical views.

SHARIA LAW

In traditional Islam there is no distinction between secular and religious life. Instructions and examples set forth in the Qur'an, the Sunnah and the Hadith can provide guidelines for nearly every aspect of day-to-day living (prayer, jurisprudence, gender roles, dietary laws, dress codes etc.) For issues that didn't exist in the 8th century (for examples, rules regarding abortion, cryogenics, organ donation, cloning etc.) the standard sources are supplemented by laws determined by popular consensus (*ijma*) and analogies (*qiyas*) comparing the modern matters to similar concerns that existed in the past.

Very conservative Muslims would like to erase the line that separates the mosque from the state by developing nations governed solely by **Sharia law**. For a time, the Taliban applied Sharia law in Afghanistan. Iran, Saudi Arabia, Sudan and, to some extent, Libya have all incorporated it in their national legal systems. Most Muslim countries, especially those that were once part of the European colonial system (Pakistan, Iraq, Lebanon etc.), have abandoned Sharia law for more modern, secular or Western, legal systems. To some fundamental Muslims, a return to Sharia law would symbolize a return to an age of faith and the complete liberation from foreign influence.

RULES OF CONDUCT

According to Islamic law, every act fits into the following categories:

Fard: Those acts that are obligatory under law, for example, the observation of the Five Pillars and participation in jihad.

Wajib: Actions that are obligatory but not expressly mentioned in the primary sources of law

Mustahabb or **Mandub:** Actions that are not obligatory but are recommended. Charitable acts and voluntary extra prayers, fasts and trips to the Holy Land (Mecca) are all Mustahabb, that is to say, not required but rewarded.

Mubah: Neutral or permitted acts.

Makruh: Actions that are not forbidden but discouraged. Divorce, for example, is frowned upon but not forbidden in Islam

Haram: Actions that are absolutely forbidden. Gambling, the consumption of alcoholic beverages or anything that intoxicates the mind; theft; illicit sexual activity are all haram (forbidden).

Halal: That which is permitted. Particularly applies to food (see Dietary Laws).

DIETARY LAWS

Muslims, like Jews, are instructed to abstain from eating certain foods in the interest of health, cleanliness and obedience to God. Although Islamic laws determining which foods are considered *halal* (permissible) or *haram* (forbidden) are very similar to Jewish kosher laws, they are less stringent and less numerous.

GENERAL
Judaism: Only foods that are explicitly permitted (*kosher*) can be eaten.

Islam: Any food that is not forbidden can be eaten.

However, both Jews and Muslims are permitted to violate dietary laws if necessary for survival.

MEAT Both Muslims and Jews prohibit the consumption of pork and blood and have rules dictating the proper way to slaughter animals.

Judaism: Only cloven-hoofed animals that chew their cud[27] can be eaten (cows, sheep, goats and deer). Pigs (pork) therefore, are forbidden. All animals must be free of defects and disease and slaughtered in a quick and merciful matter. Once killed, the animals must be washed and soaked in salt to remove the blood. Eating meat and dairy products together in the same meal is not permitted.

Islam: Animals must be slaughtered in a quick and merciful manner and drained of all their blood. Any animal that has died on its own (for example by disease, natural death, having fallen from a height, in battle with other animals etc.) cannot be eaten.

FISH AND SEAFOOD
Judaism: Only fish that have scales and fins can be consumed. Therefore, shellfish is forbidden.

Islam: All seafood is permitted.

ALCOHOL
Judaism: Not prohibited unless the alcohol has been in contact with non-kosher elements.

Islam: Alcohol and all other intoxicants are prohibited.

5:91 *Satan's plan is but to excite enmity and hatred between you, with intoxicants and gambling, and hinder you from the remembrance of God and from prayer: will ye not then abstain?*

Some Muslims interpret this and other verses to mean that all things that interfere with the clear functioning of the mind are prohibited (including street drugs, tobacco etc.)

---

[27] Food that has been brought up from the first stomach to be chewed a second time.

WOMEN

And they (women) *have rights similar to those of men over them in kindness... 2: 228 They* (women) *are a garment for you and you are a garment for them...* (2:187)

In Islam, men and women are regarded as equal sexes in the eyes of God. The Qur'an, for instance, states that **Adam** and **Eve** were created at the same time for each other's comfort (Eve wasn't created out of Adam's rib) and they were both equally blamed for eating the forbidden fruit. Islam has also taught that females should not be denied a political voice – which has allowed **Benazir Bhutto,** former Prime Minister of Muslim Pakistan, to lead her country (the United States has never had a female president). Also, women are not supposed to be denied the right to an education (many famous religious scholars [*ulema*] have been women).

However, because the two sexes are different biologically and psychologically,[28] their roles in the family differ as well. Since a man is expected to support the family, he is entitled to receive a larger inheritance than his sisters. Accordingly, a woman is entitled to keep the property she inherited or acquired as dowry.

MARRIAGE
While a man is allowed to marry up to four women, restrictions laid out in Islamic law make polygyny (marriage to many women) difficult to carry out in practice. The first wife must give her husband permission to marry again and all the wives must be treated equally, both financially and emotionally (a task which the Qur'an claims isn't feasible). In many countries, moreover, polygamy is legally banned or socially unacceptable. (Only Muhammed was authorized to marry more than four women at a time). Forced marriage is prohibited and Muslim women may only marry a Muslim while men may marry any woman who believes in the one true God (Muslim, Jewish, Christian, Zoroastrian etc.).

FIDELITY (Faithfulness)
Both a man and a woman are subject to the most severe punishment in this life and the next for infidelity. However, in order to be charged with the crime, the illicit act must have been witnessed by four people. Ruining a woman's reputation by false accusations is considered a criminal act.

DIVORCE
Although divorce is heavily discouraged, a man is allowed to unilaterally demand a divorce by stating his request three times within a period of three

---

[28] 4:34 *Men are the protectors and maintainers of women, Because God has given the one more strength than the other, and because they support them from their means. Therefore the righteous women are devoutly obedient, and guard in the husband's absence what God would have them guard.*

months (three menstrual cycles - to assure that she isn't pregnant). If the couple reconciles or engages in sexual relations during that time, the divorce is considered null and void. A man may not divorce his wife if she is pregnant. A divorced wife is entitled to continue living in her husband's house and receive good treatment.

A wife may divorce her husband under certain circumstances (abandonment, abuse, sterility etc.) with legal assistance.

SPOUSAL ABUSE
A man may discipline his wife for transgressions against his wishes. However, spousal abuse is a punishable offense. [29]

MUHAMMED AND WOMEN
Muhammed's first wife, **Khadija**, was a wealthy and powerful woman who ran her own caravan business after her first husband's death. Many years Muhammed's senior, Khadija asked the future Messenger of God to be her husband and bore him six children. Muhammed, in turn, was loyal to Khadija until her death 25 years later.

He married his second wife, **Sauda**, also a widow, a few weeks later. His third wife, **Aisha**, the daughter of his closest friend and the first caliph, **Abu Bakr**, was nine years old when he married her and was the only virgin among his wives. Aisha, Muhammed's favorite wife, was also a powerful woman who, years later, participated in a revolt against Muhammed's son-in-law, **Ali**, at the **Battle of the Camel**.

Among his other ten wives: almost all were widows (many had lost husbands in the course of Muslim battles) two were Jewish, two were daughters of his companions, one was the daughter of an enemy (**Abu Sofian**) and the last, **Mary**, was a slave girl gifted to Muhammed by the ruler of Egypt. After Khadija, Mary was the only wife after Khadija to bear him a child – a son who died at a young age.

In a time when women far outnumbered men, multiple marriages were considered a kindness rather than an indulgence since women had no opportunity to support themselves and their children. Without polygamy, widowed women and orphaned children would have perished after the death of the head of the household. In Muhammed's day, moreover, men were discouraged from having any physical contact with women who were not relatives or wives. Muhammed's "harem," therefore was less a "pleasure palace" than a community of middle-aged widows who enjoyed the Prophets company and support.

---

[29] *4:34 As to those women on whose part ye fear disloyalty and ill-conduct, admonish them first, next refuse to share their beds, and last beat them lightly. But if they return to obedience, seek not against them means of annoyance; for God is most high, Great above you all.*

MUSLIM CLOTHING

Although the restrictive *burqa*, a compulsory full-length garment with a mesh covering over the eyes worn by women living under the **Taliban** regime in Afghanistan, has mistakenly come to exemplify extreme Islamic sartorial requirements, the heavy covering only represents one interpretation of the   dress codes set out in the Qur'an and the Hadiths.

As it is written in Sura 24:30-31, *Women should lower their gaze and guard their modesty; they should not display their ornaments except as is normal, they should draw their veils over their bosoms and not display their beauty except to their close male relatives.*

Along with strictures against transparent or form-fitting clothes, these instructions aim to minimize the image of women as sex objects and to emphasize their piety, purity and chastity. Many Muslim women find this representation liberating and welcome *hijab* (literally "veil," the general term designating all proper clothing) as a way to make men notice their minds and characters rather than their physical attributes.

Liberal Muslims believe that as long as the body is modestly covered, any style of dress complies with the Qur'anic principles as set forth in the previous paragraph. Women who wear head scarves that hide their hair from public view, however, follow the **Sunnah** (or custom) of the Prophet's wives who covered themselves. More moderate women also wear a *jilbab*, a long coat or kaftan, in conformance with Muhammed's assertion that no part of a female past the age of puberty should be seen except her face and hands.

Although nowhere does the Qur'an state explicitly that the veiling of the face is required, many conservative women refer to a verse from the Qur'an which advises women to "speak to strange men (that is, not related family) through a curtain," and interpreted as a reason to cover up.

HIJAB IN HISTORY

Wearing of the face veil (along with the seclusion of women) was practiced long before the 7th century in classical Greece, Byzantium, Persia and in India among the upper caste Rajput women. During the time of the Prophet, however, the veil was hardly used at all. One of the *Hadith* even claim that **Aisha**, Muhammed's favorite wife, told the son of a companion, "the Almighty has put on me the stamp of beauty, it is my wish that the public should view the beauty and thereby recognize His grace unto them. On no account, therefore, will I veil myself."

About two centuries later, however, the use of a face covering veil was reinstated to distinguish well-to-do women (who wore restrictive clothing) from those who had to work outside the house. Hence the garments came to symbolize wealth and prestige. In the same way, a family's honor was gauged by the modesty and piety of its female members reflected in the clothes that they wore.

But just as the veil came to symbolize affluence, honor and piety, the absence of the veil in Muslim countries symbolized modernity to some rulers in the twentieth century.

When Turkey's founder **Mustafa Kemal Ataturk** began to build a secular nation-state in 1923, for instance, he denounced the use of the veil as demeaning to women and a hindrance to civilization. In Iran a few years later, **Reza Shah Pahlevi** issued a proclamation banning the veil outright in a drive to modernize the country. To many women, the sudden decree was less liberating than it was frightening, uncomfortable and offensive.

POLITICS OF THE VEIL

The veil has been a potent symbol for both reformers, who see *chadors* and *burqas* as symbols of female subjugation, and traditionalists who see *hijab* as a way to demonstrate devotion to Islam in the face of westernization and subsequent immorality.

For years, feminist groups such as the **Feminist Majority** based in the United States, pointed to the Taliban's enforcement of the *burqa* in Afghanistan as a male-chauvinistic attempt to suppress women. A few months after the Taliban had been defeated, though, most of the Afghan women continued to wear the *burqa* voluntarily, considering it to be a symbol of purity, chastity, Islamic duty and cultural identity.

TERMS

Chador

(Also called the Persian "tent") A black, loose-fitting cloak that covers the body, head and hair but not the face. After the Iranian revolution in 1979, women were required to cover their heads by scarves or to wear the chador. In Iran, every girl must cover up by the age of nine.

Burqa

The burqa is a heavier and larger version of the chador concealing the entire figure. A mesh covering for the eyes is sewn into the headpiece which is attached to a floor-length flared veil. It was commonly worn in Afghanistan during the rule of the Taliban as well as parts of Pakistan, India and on the Arabian Peninsula.

Abaya

Loose black robe from head to toe worn mostly by women in Saudi Arabia.

Khimar

Headscarf that hangs down to just above the waist.

HEAVEN AND HELL

More than a quarter of the Qur'an deals with issues of Heaven and Hell since the Muslims believe the afterlife is eternal while one's time on this earth is just a period of testing and learning. From the moment the Angel of Life breathes a soul into a fetus (about four months after conception) he or she begins to deal with the trials of life.

With the guidance provided in the books of the prophets and the examples of their infallible lifestyles, a person is encouraged to live one's lives according to the "straight path" in order to assure their souls a comfortable place in Paradise after Judgment Day.

From childhood, all of one's deeds and thoughts are recorded by angels who figuratively sit on their shoulders. The task of the angel on the right shoulder is to take note of good deeds and pious acts while the angel on the left keeps track of digressions.

After death, two more angels will ask three important questions; "Who is your Lord?" "How did you live your life?" "Who was your Prophet?" The correct answers would be: "God,"

MAHDI (lit. "the guided one")

According to early Hadith literature, at the end of times, a Mahdi (or Messiah) will appear and unite all the Schools of Law and all the Muslim sects. The Mahdi will introduce a period of peace and tranquility in anticipation of the appearance of the Antichrist *(Dajjal)* and the return of Jesus — who will then destroy the Antichrist.

In some sources, it is predicted that the Mahdi, a descendant of the Prophet, will also be called Muhammed (or a variation of the name: Ahmad, Mahmud etc.), his mother will have the name Amina (the same name as the Prophet's mother) and his father's name will be Abdullah (again like the Prophet). He will be tall with a fair complexion and will speak with a light stutter.

Twelver Shia Muslims believe the twelfth and last Imam will reappear as the Mahdi around Judgment Day after 1000 years in hiding.

"According to the will of God" and the name of one's prophet (Muhammed, Jesus, Moses, etc.)"[30] The person's records will be given to God who will decide whether they are destined for Heaven (Paradise) or Hell. The souls, which have been pulled out of every cell of the dead bodies, will then rest peacefully or in torment (depending on the score on one's life's record) near their corporal remains until the Day of Reckoning arrives.

---

[30] 10:47 *To every people was sent an Apostle: when their Apostle comes before them, the matter will be judged between them with justice and they will not be wronged.*

As God created the universe, he will also roll it up and destroy it when he pleases. For the next 50,000 years all the souls will be arranged according to belief (the Muslims will stand behind Muhammed, the Christians behind Jesus, and the Jews behind Moses for instance) and the individual books of deeds will be brought out. Those who lived good lives will be sent to Paradise, while the sinners will be banished to Hell where they will suffer alone in heat 70 times that of earth with only fountains of blood, pus and burning oil as refreshment.

In the Garden of Paradise (**Jannah**) the blessed will find gardens of bliss, eternal youth and good health, rolling meadows, exquisite cities, wine (forbidden as a mortal) and good food that is consumed purely for the joy of eating.[31] Beautiful, dark-eyed, immaculate virgins (*houris*) will serve worthy souls. Husbands and wives will be reunited (if they wish) and families and friends will socialize in an eternal blissful realm without boredom, spite, jealousy, anger or unfulfilled desire.

---

[31] 55:54 *They will recline on Carpets, whose inner linings will be of rich brocade: the Fruit of the gardens will be near and easy of reach. In them will be maidens, chaste, restraining their glances, whom no man or Jinn before them has touched.*

SECTS AND OFFSHOOTS

One of the most enduring traits of Islam is its singular devotion to God, the Qur'an and the Five Pillars of Islam (observed by all Muslims). Any division among members of the faith is prohibited in the Qur'an.

Nevertheless, as in all religions, Islam and its scriptures (Qur'an, Sunnah and Hadith), are susceptible to multiple interpretations and different degrees of observance.

The first major disagreement occurred only a few decades after the death of the Prophet (with the Shi'ite/Sunni rift after Ali's, the Prophets son-in-law, death in 661) and offshoots based loosely on the original tenets of Islam have diluted the original message so thoroughly that their Islamic roots are nearly imperceptible.

SUNNI MUSLIMS

The name "Sunni" is derived from the word "Sunnah," the way of life prescribed for Muslims based on the sayings and practices of Prophet Muhammed.

Accounting for at least 85% of all Muslims, the Sunnis acknowledged the authority of a series of caliphs (civil and religious leader of a Muslim state) beginning with **Abu Bakr**, the first caliph, the companion and friend of Prophet Muhammed. After the death in 1258 of the last official caliph, **al-Musta'sim** (who died without any heirs), the Caliphate continued as a more symbolic position until the office was abolished altogether in 1924 by the secular Turkish ruler, **Kemal Ataturk.**

SHI'A MUSLIMS

Accounting for only 10% of all Muslims, the Shi'a deviated from the Sunni believers in about A.D. 680 when **Mu'awiyya ibn Abi Sufyan** was elected as the fifth caliph over Ali's descendants. His followers called the Shi'a (short for "Shi'at Ali" or "the party of Ali") deemed all the caliphates elected from that point on as illegitimate usurpers and, though they continued to hold the same fundamental beliefs as their Muslim brothers, they developed and observed their own set of Hadith, rituals and alternative line of religious leaders (the Imams).

TWELVERS **(Ithna-Ashara)**

The Twelvers or Ithna-Ashara (the main branch of Shi'ism) followed a line of spiritual guides, called Imams beginning with Ali's son and grandson (**Hassan** and **Husayn**) and continuing through twelve descendants (hence the name "Twelvers") until **Muhammad ibn al-Hasan (Al-Mahdi-Sahibuz Zaman)**. Because al-Hasan was only five years old when his father died in A.D. 874, and because his followers feared he would be assassinated by the Sunni Caliphate,[32] the twelfth Imam was said to have been hidden by his closest deputies.

Today, the Twelvers believe that the Imam never died but is still in hiding (or "**occultation**") and will remain hidden until God commands him to reappear on Judgment Day as the Messiah or **Mahdi**. Once he returns, the Mahdi is expected to establish a reign of justice and peace on earth ushering in the return of Jesus Christ.

FIVERS (Zaidis or Zaddiyah)

After the accession of the fourth Imam, **Ali Zayn al-Abidin** the Shi'as began to split over differences in the lineage of the Imams. Fivers or Zaidis believed that **Zayd bin Ali** was the rightful successor to the Imamate rather than his half-brother, **Muhammad al-Baqir** who the Twelvers recognized as the fifth Imam.

> **12 Imams**
>
> 1) Ali ibn Abu Talib (600-661)
> 2) Hasan ibn Ali (625-669)
> 3) Husayn ibn Ali (626-680)
> 4) Ali Zayn al Abidin (658-713)
>   Fivers (Zaidis) argue that Husayn's grandson, Zayd bin Ali, Muhammad al Baqir's half-brother was the fifth Imam.
> 5) Muhammad al Baqir (676-743)
> 6) Jafar as Sadiq (703-765)
>   Seveners (Ismailis) believe that Musa al Kazim's brother Ismail was the seventh and last Imam.
> 7) Musa al Kazim (745-799)
> 8) Ali ar Rida (765-818)
> 9) Muhammad at Taqi (810-835)
> 10) Ali al Hadi (827-868)
> 11) Hasan al Askari (846-874)
> 12) Muhammad al Mahdi (868 - ?)

Also unlike the Twelvers, the Zaidis did not believe in the infallibility of the Imams nor that the line should be passed from father to son. They also reject the notion of an Imam still in hiding.

Zaidis, who make up about 40% of the population of Yemen, have more in common with Sunnis than they do with most Shi'as.

SEVENERS (Ismailis)

Like the Fivers, the Ismailis also differed with the Twelvers over the order of succession of Imams. After the death of the sixth Imam, **Jafar as Sadiq**, the Seveners claimed that his oldest son, **Ismail** (who had been passed over by Twelver Shi'as because he allegedly drank wine) had inherited the right to rule rather than his younger brother, **Musa al Kazim**.

---

[32] None of the Imams ever ruled an Islamic government but their followers hoped that they would one day assume the leadership of the Islamic community. Knowing this, Sunni Caliphs were careful to keep the Shi'as politically weak through persecution and by threats on the life of their religious leaders.

In the 10th century, an Ismaili Imam emigrated to North Africa and established the **Fatimid Dynasty** (named because the Imam, **Abdullah al-Mahdi**, was said to be descended directly from Fatima, the Prophet Muhammed's daughter and the wife of Ali). From 969 to 1171, the **Fatimids**, from their seat in Cairo,[33] ruled a vast empire that at one point included Mecca and Medina (in present-day Saudi Arabia), Palestine, Syria and North Africa and challenged the Sunni **Abbasid** Empire centered in Baghdad (present-day Iraq). The empire began to fall apart after the Crusaders captured Jerusalem in 1099.

The Ismaili group (the second largest of the Shi'a groups with 15 million adherents) itself split into factions.

ALAWI (also known as Nusayris or Ansaris)

The Alawis (literally "followers of Ali," the fourth caliph) are an off-shoot of the Ismaili branch of Shi'a Islam and make up the largest religious minority in Syria. The branch developed in the mountain regions of Syria among isolated communities that had already been influenced by the Christian Byzantines and Western Crusaders who had come through their towns. For that reason, their branch of Islam incorporates a number of Christian rituals – so many, in fact, that their religion is no longer regarded as a form of Islam by many Muslims. Although its members faithfully observe the Five Pillars and recognize Muhammed as a Prophet (although they believe that Muhammed was "created" by Ali), they also believe in reincarnation, a divine Trinity and the idea that God can be physically incarnated in the body of a human (namely Ali). According to the Alawis, all people began as stars and men (but not women) are reincarnated seven times before they will once again return to the world of light. They also believe that Ali created Muhammed who in turn created **Salman** (an early Shi'ite saint) and that Ali, Muhammed and Salman form a holy Trinity.

Like Christians (and unlike Muslims), the Alawi celebrate many of the Christian festivals including Christmas, Easter, Palm Sunday etc. and honor many Christian saints. By incorporating bread and wine (forbidden in Islam) in their ceremonies, they reveal even stronger tendencies towards Christianity.

As members of neither the Christian faith nor necessarily traditional Islam, the Alawis have suffered centuries of discrimination from both groups – that is, until one of their own, **Hafez Asad**, became the President of Syria in 1970.

---

[33] The Fatimids established the famous **Al Azhar** university in Egypt.

DRUZE (Mowahhidoon)

The Druze are another branch of Ismailis developed in Cairo in the 11th century during the reign of the sixth Ismaili Fatimid Caliph **Abu Ali al-Mansur al-Hakim** (985-1021), who they believe was endowed with god-like qualities.[34] This very secretive sect, which has about 250,000 members, also regards **Jethro, Moses'** father-in-law as a prophet and make pilgrimages to his burial place near Tiberius.

Because of their attribution of divinity to Hakim, they are considered heretics in the eyes of the Muslim community (who believe that only God is divine).

NIZARI (or Khoja – once known as Assassins)

Still another Ismaili offshoot, the **Nizari** or "**Assassins**" (possibly so-named because they smoked hashish before going into battle) developed in the 11th century and were once known for sending men on suicide missions to kill the commanders of armies that threatened their strongholds (hence the modern derivation of the word "assassin"). Over time, the group became more peaceful and moved into the Indian subcontinent. Today, the 20 million strong Khojas are led by the Aga Khan,[35] **Prince Karim**, (b. 1937) the 49th direct descendant in a male line down from Ali.

KHARIJITES (or Khawarij)

The Kharijites were the first Muslims to split away from mainstream Islam when Muhammed's son-in-law/cousin **Ali** decided to settle the question of succession to the Caliphate through human arbitration (see chapter Rightly Guided Caliphs). In protest, the Kharijites (or "dissenters"), who believed such an important decision could only be made by God, formed their own radical faction in A.D. 658.

Based in southern Iraq, the branch accounts for less than 1% of all Muslims and maintains fundamentalist views of Islam. To the Kharijites, the Muslim world can be divided into two categories: the "true Muslims," those who adhere strictly to religious rules, and "unbelievers," Muslims who strayed from what the Kharijites believed were the real directives established by Allah. Members of

---

[34] One of the early leaders of the Druze taught that the divine light and spirit embodied in **Adam** had been transmitted to **Ali** (Muhhamed's cousin) and through him and the Imams to **al-Hakim**. The Druze believe that Hakim vanished into hiding (occultation) and will one day return to inaugurate a messianic golden age.

[35] Since the 19th century, the Naziri branch of Ismailis gave their spiritual leaders the title of Aga Khan. The third Aga Khan, **Sultan Muhammad** (1877-1957) was a founder of the **All-Indian Muslim League** and played a significant role in the movement to establish the Muslim state of Pakistan. (See Roraback, Pakistan in a Nutshell, Enisen Publishing, 2004)

the sect felt that anyone who broke serious religious rules was guilty of treason and, like other outlaws, could be killed with impunity (as a Kharijite had done in A.D. 661 when he assassinated Ali). Their radical interpretations inspired some of the more extreme Muslim groups such as **Islamic Jihad**, (see chapter <u>Muslim Militants)</u> who were devoted to redirecting Muslims along the "true path" of Islam.

AHMADIYYAH (or Ahmadis)

The Ahmadi community was founded in Qadian, India in the 19th century by **Mirza Ghulam Ahmad**. In 1180, Ahmad declared himself a "renewer of faith" (*Mujaddid*)[36] and, eleven years later, claimed that he was the Mahdi (Messiah) and the last Avatar of Vishnu.[37] Some of his followers (who split into two sects — the **Qadianis** and **Lahorites**) believed that he was a prophet who should be recognized by all Muslims. Because they denied the finality of Muhammed as the last prophet (a central Islamic tenet), many Muslims believed Ahmadi ideas were too blasphemous for the group to be considered an authentic Islamic sect.

In Pakistan, in particular, the Ahmadis suffered from widespread discrimination. As "non-Muslims" the Ahmadis were forbidden to worship in non-Ahmadi mosques, use traditional Islamic greetings in public, take part in the Hajj or display any other Islamic traits in public (or risk imprisonment up to three years). As a "non-Muslim" minority, moreover, they were denied adequate representation in Pakistan's government.

SUFI

It is commonly believed that the name "sufi" came from the word "suf," the name of the simple coarse wool garment donned by mystics as a symbol of their rejection of materialism. But the word has also been linked with the root "sofos" or "sofia" meaning "wisdom" in several languages, or "saaf" meaning "pure" and "safwe," or "those who are selected."

Sufis, who are drawn from many Sunni and Shi'a schools, essentially believe and practice the core tenets of Islam. They believe that God (Allah) is the only God and Muhammed was his last prophet. They also observe the Five Pillars of Islam and read Islamic scriptures. Where they differ is in their interpretation of the relationship between a believer and God. Sufis, who are essentially mystics, believe that a Muslim can have a personal experience with God through meditation or self-discipline. Some, like the

---

[36] According to one of the Hadith, a *mujaddid* will be sent by God every hundred years in order to wake up the Muslim community and bring them back to the faith.

[37] Hindus believe that Vishnu, one of their principle deities, was manifested in the world in a series of ten earthly incarnations known as avatars. The final avatar was expected to appear at the end of the earth's present cycle.

famous "**Whirling Dervishes**" attempt to get closer to God by dancing in circles until they put themselves into an ecstatic divine trance. Other Sufi cults draw on sacred forces or saints to facilitate their communication with Allah or practice self-mutilation to liberate their spiritual essences from their bodily shells.

Initially, Sufis adopted Shi'a ideas – believing that a messianic figure will come to save Muslims from corrupt worldly rulers (particularly the leaders of the Umayyad and Abbasid Caliphates). In time, though, Sufi mysticism and practices began to appeal to Sunni Muslims from all four major Schools of Law. Today there are hundreds of mystic orders with millions of adherents from mainstream Sunni and Shi'a communities.

The original Sufis were mystics who protested against conformity and the authority of worldly leaders by adopting ascetic lifestyles and focusing on personal piety. Eventually, they became institutionalized and organized themselves into "orders" or "brotherhoods" (called *Tariqas*) headed by spiritual leaders or *sheikhs* (also Shaykhs, Shaikhs). Members of the various brotherhoods were initiated by pledging allegiance (or *bayat*) to the sheikh in a ceremony resembling one observed by Muhammed and his companions in the 7th century.

The movement particularly appealed to disenfranchised Muslims living in rural areas because it integrated many of their folk traditions: for example, by allowing celebrations of Muhammed's birthday, permitting dancing during prayer, setting up shrines to "Islamic saints" etc. The syncretic quality of Sufism also helped spread Islam to non-Muslim areas by facilitating a slow transition from indigenous practices to the religion of Muhammed. Sufis, therefore, became effective missionaries.

But the same qualities that drew non-believers into the Islamic fold, also generated hostility among fundamental Muslims who felt the alien rituals corrupted Allah's true message.

WAHHABIS (Salafists or Muwahhidun)
Some of the most bitter opponents of Sufism, Shiism and all rituals that appear to venerate anyone or anything other than God are members of the Wahhabi movement. Adherents even object to the name "Wahhabi" since it intimates that the group follows or reveres their founder, **Ibn Abd ul-Wahhab** (1703-1792). Instead, the **Wahhabis** refer to themselves as **Muwahhidun** ("unitarians") or **Salafis** (from the phrase "*salaf as-salihin*" or "the pious ancestors") as well as the *ad dawa lil tawhid* (or "call to unity") since the movement emphasizes the essential "oneness of God" or *tawhid*.

The Salafi reform movement was started in the 18th century by **Ibn Abd ul-Wahhab** to purge all cultural practices in Muslim communities that Wahhab believed were contrary to the "straight path" of Islam. Particularly troubling to him and his followers was the practice of polytheism or *shirk*, (demonstrated by the worship of Muslim saints, the veneration of trees and stones etc.) and the idolization of human beings (by visiting gravesites and making pilgrimages to tombs, for instance). He was also disturbed by the growing laxity he observed among the Muslim community in adhering to Islamic law and the tendency of people to put luxury ahead of piety.

As a member of the Sunni **Hanbali** School of Law, (see chapter on Islamic Jurisprudence) Wahhab shared many of that school's positions including a fanatic intolerance of views other than his own, the strict literal translation of the Qur'an and the ultimate desire to create a pure Islamic state by imposing **Sharia Law** at the state level.

In order to effectively implement his ideas, Wahhab made a political alliance with a local chieftain, **Muhammed ibn Saud** by presenting a *bayat* (or oath of allegiance) and giving him his daughter in marriage. The close relationship between the two families was maintained until the 19th century when one of Saud's descendents, **Abdul Aziz bin Abdul Rahman ibn Faisal Al Saud** became the first monarch of Arabia (which was then renamed Saudi Arabia). The popularity of the Wahhabism movement progressed as the influence of **Abdul Aziz** and the Saud family grew, especially after oil was discovered on the Arabian Peninsula in 1938.

As the enforcers of Wahhabi ideology, the Saudi royal family imposed a number of laws intended to maintain the strict observance of the Wahhabi version of **Sharia Law**.[38] Considered draconian by Western standards, Saudi laws strictly adhere to Islamic principles. Adultery is punishable by death (although four witnesses to the act must swear to have witnessed the crime), as is renunciation of Islam. Repeated theft is punishable by amputation of the right hand. Offenses against religion and public morality, such as drunkenness and gambling and the neglect of prayer requirements are punished by flogging. To ensure compliance to proper Islamic protocol (observance of prayer, modest dress – women must wear headscarves and black robes or *abayas*, men are forbidden to wear gold or garments of silk – and other Islamic rules) the Saudi government employs a visible religious police force (or ***mutawwiin***).

---

[38] According to Article 23 of the Saudi Arabian constitution, it is the state's duty to "protect Islam, implement its Sharia and order people to do right and shun evil. It fulfills the duty regarding God's call." Article 7 states that the Government of Saudi Arabia "derives power from the Holy Qur'an and the Prophet's tradition."

BAHAI

In the 19th century, a Persian Shi'ite called **Siyyid Ali Muhammad** assumed the title of **Bab** (the "Gate") and declared that he was sent to usher in the hidden Messiah. After Ali Muhammad's execution in 1850, one of his followers, **Baha'ullah** or **Baha Allah**, declared that he, himself was the Messiah prophesied by all religions and became the head of a new movement.

From that time on the movement diverged so far away from Islam that it became an entirely separate religion with its own scriptures and principles.

Like Muslims (and Christians and Jews), the Bahais believe that there is only one God and that He created the universe. They also believe that all religions developed from a singular source and were influenced by a series of prophets sent by God including Adam, Abraham, Moses, Krishna, Zoroaster, Buddha, Jesus, Muhammed, the Bab and finally Baha'ullah.

NATION OF ISLAM

In 1913, **Timothy Drew**, a black American born to a Moroccan Muslim father and a Native American mother founded the **Moorish Science Temple of America** based on the belief that blacks were of Moorish[39] descent and therefore had Muslim origins.

One of his followers, **Wallace Fard Muhammad** (1877-1931?) expounded on the theory by adding that blacks were racially superior to whites and that the Christian Church was historically the religion of an oppressing white race. His **Nation of Islam** movement (also called the **Black Muslim Movement** or BMM), attracted a number of disciples including **Elijah Poole** (1897-1975).

After W.F. Muhammad's mysterious disappearance in 1931, Poole, who changed his name to **Elijah Muhammad**, declared that Wallace Fard Muhammad was God incarnate and assumed leadership of the NOI movement.

From his jail cell, a prisoner called **Malcolm Little** learned about Elijah Muhammad's teachings and became a member of the NOI himself after his release in 1952. Soon after joining the Nation of Islam, Malcolm changed his last name to X in order to erase the influence that his slave owners had over his ancestors by creating their surname. After a fateful trip to Mecca in 1964 in observation of the Islamic Pillar to make a pilgrimage to the holy city in one's lifetime, **Malcolm X** was transformed. In Mecca he prayed equally with Muslim men of every race and came home feeling he had been wrong to condemn people based on their color.

---

[39] Moors are African Muslims of Berber and Arab descent.

Islam in a Nutshell

When he returned to America, he broke with the hard line Nation of Islam and formed his own **Organization of Afro-American Unity**. A year later, he was assassinated.

After the death of Elijah Muhammad, his son **Warith Deen Muhammad** took over the leadership of the NOI, rejected his father's black separatist views, denied the claim that Elijah Muhammad was a divine messenger, brought the movement closer to Sunni Islam and renamed it the **Muslim American Society.**

His changes enraged a number of NOI followers including the American calypso singer and actor, **Louis Eugene Walcott** (renamed **Louis X** and then **Louis Farrakhan**) who believed that he should have been Elijah's successor. In 1981, Farrakhan announced the restoration of the old Nation of Islam and led his own spin-off version espousing the original tenets of black supremacism and adherence to an ethical code that included abstaining from smoking, alcohol, drugs, sports, movies, cosmetics and the consumption of pork.

In accordance with mainstream Muslims, the members of the Nation of Islam believe that there is only one all-powerful God; that believers should fast during the holy month of Ramadan and that they should acknowledge the Qur'an as their primary source of scriptural teachings. The NOI differs from Islam in rejecting the notion that Muhammed was the last prophet believing instead that God's message was also sent through Elijah Muhammed and Farrakhan. Contrary to Islam, NOI also teaches that one race is superior to another. In Islam, all races are equal in the eyes of God.

ROOTS OF ISLAMIC MILITANCY

Since the earliest schisms in the Islamic religion, Muslims have differed in their practice of Islamic rituals and their interpretations of the Holy Scriptures. Yet despite the slight doctrinal differences, for the last 1300 years, the Muslim community has been more or less unified under the Caliphs (from the **Umayyad** to the **Abbasid** Dynasty) or Sultans (heading the **Ottoman Empire** from 1380-1918) who ruled over vast empires.

But with the dissolution of the Ottoman Empire in 1918 and the European mandate[40] that followed, the Islamic community became disjointed. After the breakup of the Ottoman Empire, some Muslim countries assimilated with their European occupiers by adopting Western conventions and styles of governance (as Iraq has done for example). Some enforced the ancient traditions of the Prophet by legally implementing **Sharia Law** (Saudi Arabia and Iran).[41] Other nations adopted some Western ideas and set up token Sharia courts to arbitrate family law alongside Western-style courts.

As Western culture and ideologies continued to penetrate into Muslim areas, Islam appeared to be at risk of corruption by "foreign ideas." In reaction, some conservative Muslims began to look for ways to lead the Muslim community back to the "straight path" of Islam while blocking the infiltration of Western thought.

SAYED ABUL ALA MAUDUDI (or Mawdudi) (1903-1979)

Maududi was an Islamic thinker and writer who was based in the Indian subcontinent when it was under the imperial rule of Britain.[42] Maududi, who was influenced by **Deobandi** ideology (see Islamic Jurisprudence), believed that Islam was in danger of being destroyed by the power of the West and called on all Muslims to protect it.

In his view, man-made laws only benefited the corrupt rulers who made them and were not worthy of obedience. Sharia law, on the other hand, came directly from God and, therefore, was pure and perfect.

"To acknowledge the personal authority of a human being as a source of commands and prohibitions," he explained in his book Jihad in Islam, "is tantamount to admitting him as the sharer in the Powers of Authority of God.

---

[40] After WWI territories that were once part of the Ottoman Empire were put under the tutelage of Britain and France (the mandate system) until they were able to govern themselves. Countries included: Syria, Palestine, Lebanon, Jordan, Iraq.

[41] After World War II many newly independent Muslim countries included provisions in their constitutions declaring that Islam be the official religion of the state or mandating that the president of the republic must be a Muslim.

[42] After its independence from Britain in 1948, India divided into two states: the Muslim state of Pakistan (itself divided into Bangladesh in the east and Pakistan in the west) and the primarily Hindu state of India. See Pakistan in a Nutshell.

And this is the root of all evils in the universe."

To Maududi, all Muslims had a duty to engage in *jihad* (in this case interpreted as "holy war") in order to recreate their societies and ultimately the world by eliminating secular or un-Islamic rule and establishing a pure Islamic system of state rule.

To institutionalize his revolutionary platform, Maududi founded **Jamaat-i-Islami** ("Islamic Party") in 1941. His many writings on Islam have since been translated into 40 languages and have influenced fundamental Muslims worldwide.

In 1951, his works were published in Egypt at a time when the drive towards Islamization was beginning to develop.

MUSLIM BROTHERHOOD

The Muslim Brotherhood was founded by **Hasan al-Banna** in Egypt in 1928 and later spread throughout the Muslim world. Like Maududi, its members advocated a return to Sharia law and advocated *jihad* against all those who do not follow Islam since, according to Banna, "Muslim lands have been trampled over and their honor besmirched."

This radical group was particularly disturbed by secular trends in Muslim governments and found itself in conflict with Egyptian President **Gamal abdul Nasser** in the 1950s. The Brotherhood had already been implicated in many assassinations by 1954 when Nasser accused the group of plotting his death and imprisoned its key members.

By the 1970s the Brotherhood had separated into peaceful, moderate and radical splinter groups. In 1981, one of the more militant factions, the **Egyptian Islamic Jihad**, was responsible for the assassination of Nasser's successor, **Anwar Sadat** after he agreed to a peace treaty with Israel at **Camp David** in Maryland.

SAYYID QUTB (1906-1966)

Sayyid Qutb was one of the Muslim Brotherhood's most distinguished intellectuals, and a hero to many of the militants who eventually joined Al-Qaeda. As a child, he received a traditional Muslim education and reportedly memorized the Qur'an by age 10. In the 1940s Qutb spent time in the United States, earning a master's degree at Colorado State College. The trip is said to have made a great impression on Qutb, who was disturbed by America's sexual freedoms and materialism.

When he returned to Egypt, Qutb joined the Muslim brotherhood and was among the core members who were arrested in 1954. In prison he wrote his seminal book called <u>Milestones</u> which became a manifesto to Islamic fundamentalists. The book followed his 1952 commentary on the Qur'an called <u>In the Shade of the Qur'an</u> in which Qutb discussed Islamic issues such as the direction of prayer, rules for divorce, charity, crime and punishment, dietary regulations, liquor, clothing etc.

In his books Qutb theorized that mankind was miserable, anxious and skeptical because it was living a schizophrenic lifestyle split between modernity and man's truest nature. As a result, people were turning to drugs, alcohol and existentialism.

The cause of this split, he claimed, came from the Christian church, which was responsible for separating the spiritual world from the secular world.

According to Qutb God sent his first set of guidelines to the Jews rhough **Moses** instructing them how to eat, dress, pray and generally how to behave in every sphere of life. By observing these laws, the Jews could live a worldly existence that was also at one with God. Eventually, though, the religion began to wither as the system of rituals became rigid and lifeless. In response, God sent another prophet, **Jesus**, to present a reformed set of guidelines such as lifting some of the dietary restrictions.

In Qutb's opinion, Jesus' disciples, though, took the rejection of Jewish teachings too far and discarded most of Moses' original laws on sex, dress, marriage etc. In the end, the Christians formed a separate religion and, under the influence of the Roman Emperor **Constantine,** began to separate laws regarding worldly affairs from those dictating one's spiritual responsibilities. This division created a sense of split personality, or "schizophrenia," that was frozen into church teachings until modern time (manifested especially in the Western ideal of "separation of church and state").

In the 7th century, God delivered yet another revelation through Prophet **Muhammed** to reestablish a correct, integrated set of spiritual/secular guidelines for the world. In the Qur'an, he even instructed man to be his vicegerent[43] and to take charge of the physical world (which the early Muslims did by studying the nature of the world through scientific inquiry).

As the Islamic world became more complacent and secular, however, it began to weaken allowing the liberal Western world to infiltrate it through the Crusades, European imperialism, the creation of Israel and the introduction of decadent Western culture. In the process, the foreigners also inflicted their "hideous schizophrenia" on people and cultures across the globe.

Qutb's remedy: Once Muslims realize the danger that Islam is facing from within and from outside the Muslim world, they must take action. As vanguards,[44] the true Muslims must fight to resurrect the Caliphate and take

---

[43] Vicegerent: a person appointed by another to exercise the latter's power and authority. 2:30 *Behold the Lord said to the angels: 'I will create a vicegerent on earth.*

[44] Fighters in the army who go ahead of the main body in an advance.

Islam to the world by reinstating **Sharia** as the legal code for all of society. Once Sharia is in place, people will finally be liberated from their enslavement under man-made laws designed by mere mortals. Secular leaders will become obsolete (only religious leaders who are entrusted with the interpretation of God's law will have any authority) and people will finally live an integrated life under God.

To his admirers, Qutb died a martyr in 1966 in Egypt at the hands of Nasser's executioners. His brother, **Muhammad Qutb**, moved to Saudi Arabia, where he taught Islamic studies at **King Abdul Aziz University** in Jedda, the school where **Osama bin Laden** was educated.

DR. SHEIKH ABDULLAH AZZAM (or Azam, Assam) (1941-1989)
Another teacher at **Abdul Aziz University, Abdullah Azzam,** was born in a village in the West Bank in Israel in 1941and joined the Palestinian **Muslim Brotherhood** in his youth. In the 1960s he joined the battle in Jordan against Israeli occupation but abandoned the Palestinian cause because he felt the fighters were too far removed from "real Islam." Soon after, he moved to Saudi Arabia to teach.

In Saudi Arabia, Azzam became convinced that the only way the Islamic nation would be victorious in its goal to reinstate the Caliphate would be to set up an organized military force.

AFGHANISTAN WAR
In 1979, Azzam had the perfect opportunity to practice what he preached when the Soviets invaded Afghanistan. To fight for his cause, the teacher left his position at Abdul-Aziz University and traveled to Pakistan near the border with Afghanistan. There he set up the **Office of Services of the Holy Warriors** (*Mujahideen*) and successfully recruited thousands of Muslim fighters from around the world to participate in the liberation of Afghanistan from the infidels.

Abdullah Azzam was instrumental in bringing discontented Muslims together resulting in the commingling of **pan-Islamist** ideas. Many of the groups eventually joined **Osama bin Laden's** international **al-Qaeda** movement creating a global network of *jihadists.*.

The victory of the *mujahideen* (sometimes called the "Afghan Arabs") over the behemoth Soviet Union[45] (albeit with help from the United States and other nations) inspired radical Islamists in all corners of the world. However, Azzam was not favored by everyone. In 1989, the Sheikh and two of his sons were assassinated.

---

[45] Muslim fighters believe that the defeat of the U.S.S.R. in Afghanistan was partly responsible for the collapse of the Soviet Union in 1991.

OSAMA BIN LADEN

Osama bin Laden was born in Saudi Arabia in 1957 to a Yemeni billionaire who worked as the chief constructor for the Saudi royal family. In 1970, Osama (the 17th child of more than 50 siblings) inherited 80 million dollars which he built into hundreds of millions of dollars and used to help fund *mujahiddin* fighters in Afghanistan.

In college (**King Abdul-Aziz University** in Jeddah), Bin Laden was inspired by the teachings of **Qutb** (whose brother taught at the university) and **Dr. Sheikh Abdullah Azzam**, a Palestinian teacher and major figure in the **Muslim Brotherhood**. Living under Saudi rule, he was also influenced by **Wahhabi** ideology (see <u>Sects and Offshoots</u>) and became immersed in the ideals of **pan-Islamicism** and the goal of reinstalling a Muslim Caliphate that would rule according to Sharia Law.

When the Soviet "infidels" (so-called by Muslims because of their atheist, communist principles) invaded Afghanistan in 1979, Bin Laden eagerly joined Azzam, his former teacher, and assisted the *mujahideen* (Muslim *jihad* fighters) by donating money and machinery to the cause.

After the assassination of his mentor, **Sheikh Azzam**, Bin Laden took over his branch of the **Muslim Brotherhood** and organized the Afghan *mujahideen* volunteers into the **al-Qaeda** (meaning "base" in Arabic) movement. This international terrorist group (which continued to grow through a series of interlocking networks with other Islamic militant cells in more than 40 countries) was believed to have been responsible for a number of attacks including the 1993 World Trade Center Bombing, the 1998 Embassy bombings in Kenya and Tanzania, the September 11, 2001 suicide plane attacks on New York City that destroyed the Twin Towers and attacks in Riyadh, Saudi Arabia in 2003. The group is also affiliated with the Egyptian **Islamic Jihad** and is believed to have links with militant groups in Kashmir, Uzbekistan, Chechnya, the Philippines and elsewhere.

TALIBAN

The departure of the Soviet forces from Afghanistan left a leadership vacuum that was quickly filled by a number of competing tribal warlords. While regional fighting was keeping Afghanistan in a state of chaos a group of **Deobandi** pupils was studying in *madrassas* (religious schools) in Pakistan. Under the leadership of their most influential member, **Mullah Muhammed Omar** and with the financial backing of **Osama bin Laden,** the Pakistan and Saudi governments and other foreign patrons, the **Taliban** (meaning "religious students") entered Afghanistan and implemented their own very strict version of **Sharia law**. Under **Taliban** rule, women were forced to cover themselves with heavy *burqas* (full body garments with mesh opening at the eyes), women were prohibited from working or studying, TVs, movies, multi-colored signs, non-religious music and flying kites were forbidden and harsh punishments were carried out for offenses such as adultery (stoning) and theft (amputation).

The Taliban was forced to disband after American and allied forces waged a war against them and took over the country in October 2001 in retaliation for the attacks on the U.S in 2001.[46]

HAMAS (or Islamic Resistance Movement)

Hamas (meaning "zeal" in Arabic and the acronym for **Harakat al-Muqawama al-Islamiya** ("Islamic Resistance Movement")) was also an offshoot of the **Muslim Brotherhood**. The Islamic group, which is devoted to the liberation of Palestine from the Zionists of Israel, opposes the policies of the secular **Palestine Liberation Organization** (PLO) and **Yasser Arafat**. Because it is also the biggest charitable organization in Palestine, it receives a lot of financial support from Muslims around the world who contribute as part of their Islamic requirement to give alms (*zakat*).

Today, the military wing of Hamas is called the **Abdullah Azzam Brigades** after the Sheikh who had inspired Bin Laden and the Afghan *mujahideen*.

---

46 For more about the Taliban, please see Roraback, Afghanistan in a Nutshell, Enisen Publishing, 2004

ISLAM and TERRORISM

Most Muslims believe one of the greatest crimes committed by the terrorists is their misrepresentation of Islam. As long as the terrorists justify their actions by attributing them to Qur'anic directives, they foster hatred for a religion that is already misunderstood in the West. For the vast majority of peaceful Muslims, their faith is a religion of peace, tolerance and love. Even the word "Islam" derives from the word meaning "peace" in Arabic.

ISLAMIC ARGUMENTS AGAINST TERRORISM:

Islam defends freedom of thought

According to the Qur'an, human beings are endowed with free will and have the power to choose or reject God. If after learning about God and the prophets, a person still chooses to reject Him and His message, then only God has the authority to judge and punish.

Muslims are very clearly instructed never to force religion on the people.

2:256 *Let there be no compulsion in religion: Truth stands out clear from error: whoever rejects evil and believes in God hath grasped the most trustworthy hand-hold, that never breaks.*

10:99 *If it had been thy Lord's will, they would all have believed ..*

8:22 *Thou art not one to manage men's affairs...*

However:

A Muslim can and should *"invite all to the way of thy Lord"* but only *"with wisdom and beautiful preaching."* (16:125)

God forbids the murder of innocent people

Killing an innocent person (as terrorists do regularly when they bomb civilian targets) is one of the gravest sins in Islam. The Qur'an equates the killing of just one guiltless person with the annihilation of all mankind.

5:32 *If anyone slew a person – unless it be for murder or for spreading mischief in the land – it would be as if he slew the whole people.*

Islam is a religion of compassion

The Qur'an regularly enjoins followers to treat people with kindness and compassion.

4:36: *....Do good – to parents, kinsfolk, orphans, those in need, neighbors who are near, neighbors who are strangers, the companion by your side, the way-farer ye meet, and what your right hand possess[es] [slaves].*

Fighting must only be defensive

The Qur'an recognizes that war is inevitable and even an obligation if it is for the purpose of ending oppression and suffering (as in the case of the early Muslims who were harassed and abused by the pagans of Mecca). But war must only be defensive and be fought justly. In all battles, the rights of the innocent and the defenseless must be protected.

22:39: *To those against whom war is made, permission is given to fight, because they are wronged...*

2:190: *Fight in the cause of God those who fight you, but do not transgress limits, for God loveth not transgressors.*

Suicide is forbidden in Islam
The Qur'an specifically deems suicide a sin.

4:29 ... *do not kill or destroy yourselves.*

2:195 .. *And make not your own hands contribute to your destruction...*

Islam is not anti-Semitic
Muhammed is believed to have been the last prophet of God following Abraham, Moses, David, Jesus and others. For that reason, the prophets and messages that God sent before Muhammed must not be denied or rejected. To do so would be tantamount to rejecting the Qur'an.

Since Muslims and the "**People of the Book**," (or those who abide by the Divine Books that were revealed by God – namely Jews and Christians), essentially share the same faith, they should all be respected.

Although God's Apostles were sent with different missions, it says in the Qur'an, each prophet should be treated with equal esteem.

2:285 *The Apostle believeth in what hath been revealed to him from his Lord, as do the men of faith. Each one of them believeth in God, His angels, His books, and His apostles. 'We make no distinction, (they say) between one and another of His apostles'...*

29:46 *Dispute ye not with the People of the Book, except with means better than mere disputation, unless it is with those of them who inflict wrong and injury; but say, 'We believe in the Revelation which has come down to us and in that which came down to you; Our God and your God is one; and it is to Him we bow in Islam [submission].*

Anti-Semitism, moreover, is a racist concept which is totally contrary to Islam. According to the Qur'an, all People of the Book will go to heaven.

2:62: *Those who believe in the Qur'an, and those who follow the Jewish scriptures and the Christians and the Sabians, any who believe in God and the Last Day, and work righteousness, shall have their reward with their Lord: on them shall be no fear, nor shall they grieve.*

According to the Muslim militants, their war is against "Zionists" not "Jews" since, in their view, Zionists (that is, Jews who support the creation of a homeland for Jews in Palestine), occupied Muslim territory and aim to eradicate Islam.

And:
5:8 *Let not the hatred of others to you make you swerve to wrong and depart from justice. Be just: that is next to piety: and fear God.*

GLOSSARY

Caliph — (or khalifa) Successor to Muhammed. The Caliphate came to an end in 1924.

Fard — rituals that are obligatory to all Muslims.

Gabriel — One of God's angels. Intermediary between God and Muhammed.

Hadith — Collection of sayings and deeds that have been attributed to Muhammed.

Hajj — Obligatory pilgrimage to Mecca (also applies to optional pilgrimages to Kerbala [Shi'a only], Jerusalem etc.)

Halal — Activities permitted by all Muslims.

Haram — Activities forbidden to all Muslims

Harem — (Literally "forbidden space"). Area where women are assured privacy in the home.

Hijab — (literally "veil") The general term designating all proper clothing.

Hijrah — Muhammed's A.D. 622 migration from Mecca to Medina (Yathrib). Designated the beginning of the Islamic calendar by Caliph Umar.

Ibn — Arabic "son of."

Imam — Literally the leader of the congregation (used by both Sunnis and Shi'as). The Sunni Muslims view the caliph as a temporal leader only and consider an imam to be a prayer leader. For Shi'as the caliphs were only de facto rulers while the rightful leadership continued to be passed along through the succession of Muhammad's descendants, the Imams. An Imam (with a capitalized "m") refers to the Shi'a descendant of the House of Ali.

Islam — Literally "submission" or "surrender" from the word *salam* meaning "peace. " The religion revealed to the Prophet Muhammed.

Jannah — Paradise (Heaven).

Jihad — Literally "striving" for God militarily, socially and personally.

Ka'aba — Cube-shaped shrine built by Abraham and Ishmail in Mecca. On the outside of one corner is the sacred Black Stone, kissed by pilgrims. The angel Gabriel gave the Black Stone to Abraham, according to one Islamic tradition; according to another, the stone was set in place by Adam.

Madrassa — (or Madrasah, Madrasa) Religious school.

Mahdi — ("Messiah") The last "hidden" Imam who will reappear on Judgment Day (Twelver Shi'a).

Mecca — Islam's most sacred city, located in what is now western Saudi Arabia. Mecca is the birthplace of Muhammed and the site of the Ka'aba

Medina — Located in western Saudi Arabia, Medina is Islam's second holiest place. Muhammed migrated to Medina with 70 Muslim families in 622 after being persecuted by the Meccan establishment (Called the "Hijrah"). It is also the site of Muhammed's tomb.

Minaret — Tower from which muezzin calls the faithful to prayer.

Mosque — The Arabic word is *masjid*, meaning "place of prostration" before God. Muhammed built the first mosque in Medina. A mosque should be oriented toward Mecca. In many of the world's Islamic societies, mosques serve social and political functions in addition to religious ones.

Muezzin — Person who calls the faithful to prayer

Mujaheddin — (Or Mujahedeen, Mujahideen) Person who engages in a jihad.

Muslim — In Arabic, "one who surrenders to God"; a follower of Islam. There are more than a billion Muslims in the world.

Purdah — The general term for the seclusion of women.

Qibla — Direction of prayer (towards Mecca).

Qur'an — (or "Koran" lit. "recitation") Islam's holy book – revelations sent by God to Muhammed beginning in the year A.D. 610.

Ramadan — 9th month in the Muslim calendar during which all believers must fast.

Riba — Interest on loaned money - forbidden in Islam.

Sharia — (or Shariah) Islamic law.

Shi'a — (or Shi'ah, Shi'ites). Followers of one of the two main branches of Islam who acknowledge only Ali and the descendants of his marriage with the Prophet's daughter Fatima as legitimate leaders of the entire community.

Shirk — Polytheism or the act of associating any person or object with powers that should be attributed only to God -- considered one of the gravest sins in Islam.

Sufi — Religious mystic. The name comes from the woolen robe (*suf*) traditionally worn by members.

Sultan — Among Mamelukes, Seljuqs and Ottomans, the customary title of the ruler who stood immediately under the caliph in the hierarchy.

Sunnah — the Prophet's example. The oral tradition of the life, deeds and sayings of the Prophet Muhammed.

Sura — (or Surah) One of the 114 chapters comprising the Qur'an.

Ulema — Religious scholars

Umma — (or Ummah) The family or community of all Muslims.

Wahhabism — A puritanical form of Islam that flourishes primarily in Saudi Arabia. It is named after Muhammed ibn al-Wahhab, an 18th-century Islamic reformer who wanted to return Islam to its beginnings by emphasizing a literalistic approach to the Qur'an.

Zakat – (or Zakah) Religious tax or alms.

******

Other books by Amanda Roraback

Aghanistan in a Nutshell
Iraq in a Nutshell
Pakistan in a Nutshell
Israel-Palestine in a Nutshell

Please look for future Nutshell Notes:
"Iran in a Nutshell," "Korea in a Nutshell," "Judaism in a Nutshell," "Mexico in a Nutshell," "Indonesia in a Nutshell," "China in a Nutshell" etc.

For more information about Enisen Publishing and for additional information about Islam, please visit www.enisen.com.

Note: English translations of the Qur'an taken from
The Holy Qur'an: Text, Translation and Commentary by Abdullah Yusuf Ali
Published by Tahrike Tarsile Qur'an, Inc, NY, 2002